AF732596

THE UNITED STATES ARMY

FROM THE EYES OF A

"MAN"

WHO OTHERS JUST

SEE AS A

"BLACK MAN"

RONNIE ISOM

SFC (Retired)

THE UNITED STATES ARMY FROM THE EYES OF A "MAN"WHO OTHERS JUST SEE AS A "BLACK MAN"

This book or parts thereof may not be reproduced in any form, stored in a retrieval system or transmitted in any form by any means – electronic, mechanical, photo copy, recording or otherwise – without prior written permission of the publisher, except as provided by United States of America copyright law.

All Rights Reserved

Copyright © 2004 by Ronnie Isom

Book design by Ronnie Isom

Library of Congress Control Number: 2004093455

International Standard Book Number: 0-9755338-0-0

Printed in the United States of America

TABLE OF CONTENTS

DEDICATED TO 5

SINCERE THANKS 6

DEEP APPRECIATION 7

***THANKS* 8**

WORDS FROM THE AUTHOR 9

***PRELUDE* 10**

***INTRODUCTION* 11**

I. FOUNDATION – MY CHILDHOOD 15

II. *A YOUNG BLACK MAN ENTERS BASIC TRAINING* 19

III. *THE JOURNEY BEGINS: GERMANY* 26

IV. THROUGHOUT ALL THE TURMOIL 30

V. *COMING BACK TO THE UNITED STATES* 33

VI. THE BATTLE: UNIFORM CODE OF MILITARY JUSTICE 36

VII. *TIME FOR CHANGE: REPORTING TO THE SIGNAL BATTALION* 39

VIII. *THE WEDDING IN THE MAKING* 41

IX. *EDUCATION FINALLY COMES: PRIMARY LEADERSHIP DEVELOPMENT COURSE* 46

X. *ON THE ROAD AGAIN: FOREIGN LAND OF GERMANY* 49

XI. *A 'BOUT' WITH RACISM* 51

XII. *THE UNIT'S MISSIONS HEATS UP* 53

XIII. *SEEING MY LIFE CHANGING - SECOND IN CHARGE (POWER)* 57

XIV. ***FORT BRAGG, North Carolina (START OF A DYNASTY)*** **63**

XV. THE INNER DESIRE TO DO SOMETHING GREAT- A NEW ERA DAWNING FAST **67**

XVI. ***THE ATTACK ON JULY 25,1990- I WAS HOT-HEADED*** **72**

XVII. ***THE YEARS 1989 THROUGH 1991: MOMENTS OF CHANGE*** **78**

XVIII. ***EMOTIONAL STATE OF MIND: FACING IT ALL*** **82**

XIX. ***THE FIGHT FOR MY LIFE- DOCUMENTING THE FACTS*** **84**

XX. ***THE TIME WAS FAST APPROACHING FULL OF ANXIETIES- PATIENCE IN DEMAND*** **90**

XXI. ***TIME TO MOVE ON: 112 SIGNAL BATTALION*** **94**

XXII. ***DREAM AND VISION MEET TOUGH RESISTANCE/OPPOSITION*** **96**

XXIII. ***TIME TO ATTACK RACISM HEADS TO HEAD*** **98**

XXIV. ***TURNING POINT - UNDERSTANDING IT ALL: EXPERIENCES*** **101**

XXV. ***NEW ERA - THE SENIOR YEARS: MATURITY*** **105**

XXVI. ***HARDSHIPS ON THE WAY: KOREA*** **108**

XXVII. ***HOME OF THE AIR ASSAULT: FT. CAMPBELL KY*** **114**

XXVIII. ***REALITY - BREAKDOWN: UNITED STATES ARMY (RACIAL PROFILE)*** **117**

XXIX. ***THE REALITY OF HIDDEN RACISM*** **120**

XXX. ***RACISM EXPERIENCES SHARED*** **123**

XXXI. ***THE FINAL ATTACK - CONSPIRACY IN FULL MOTION*** **126**

XXXII. ***CONCLUSION TO THE VISION APRIL 27 - 1735 (FINAL THOUGHTS)*** **132**

XXXIII. ***REVELATION: THE FINAL ANALYSIS*** **135**

"DEDICATED TO"

To my loving wife, "Bernice Isom" who was there through the years allowing me to serve my country well. It was through her deep dedication to keep the household that enabled me to achieve the goal of retirement. During the years, she has been there to challenge me in her own way to look within myself for the solutions to the many challenges I faced. Despite not knowing all the time what I was facing, I could always feel her genuine concern for me to overcome the many adversities. The love and tender care that she rendered to the four kids of this marriage has been beyond reproach.

It is with all my heart and soul that I dedicate this book to the woman of my life: Bernice Isom.

"SINCERE THANKS"

To my darling four kids who during these years allowed me to serve my country without having any serious incidents to deal with. Their level of discipline allowed me to concentrate on my professional career. It is with great pleasure that I again say thanks to ***Johnathon, Jason, Jessica and Jasmine Isom.*** It is with great gratitude that I am able to do this book with a great appreciation for their love and support during my 20-Year United States Army career. As they each leave to make their mark on this world, I pray they do that through being who they are. I pray that they know they are Black and should be proud of that fact. Yet I challenge each of them to strive to make their mark through the contents of their hearts and character within. Life to them will offer greater challenges and I stand tall in knowing that each of them have the rearing to meet those challenges one by one and come out victorious. As each leave, I commend them into the hands of my Lord and savior, Jesus Christ.

"DEEP APPRECIATION"

I would like to extend a deep appreciation to the following:

John W. Isom & Mary E. Isom

My Father and Mother taught me how to work hard and respect those who are older than I. It was that teaching that allowed me to maintain a high level of professionalism during my tenure of duty in the United States Army. With their strict rearing, I was foundered enough to endure the many dilemmas I faced during my Military career. Despite all the material things that I did not have as I grew up, I had the most important thing: Love. To be able to experience love and yet get the strict rearing and teaching we received growing up led me into a deeper level of being able to cope with the hardtimes of life. All that the United States Army and life brought my way after July 23, 1980 was endured as a true soldier who had been trained in the best of environments: The Country. **The life I now enjoy is deeply attributed to the fact that I was taught to be grateful for whatever state you were in. I know now without a shadow of doubt that my rearing and obedience to that rearing and God is why I am in the state I am in right now. Praise God for both of my parents.**

"THANKS"

The many **Personnel Staff Non-commissioned Officers (PSNCOs)** that served with me throughout the years. Especially those who served with me in the Foreign Land of **Korea** and my "man" in the Land of Air Assault, **Fort Campbell, KY**. You all made my job easy and led me into a deeper level of conviction in standing up for right in the midst of the opposing forces, which were many. Knowing that you had a great supporting cast made it easier for me to perform in my latter days as Senior Noncommissioned Officer in the United States Army.

All the soldiers who so diligently worked under the guidance of what many called a controversial Non-commissioned Officer. It was because of those solders that I strive so hard to be the "absolute expert". You all made me become what I lived to be today: a **"TRANSFORMER" I always wanted to leave a piece of myself with each of you and I thank you for being the willing vessels to accept that part from such a controversial Noncommissioned officer in the United States Army.**

Finally to all my many friends who were there during hard time to make me smile when all was going bad. The values of my peers, subordinates, and the superiors are beyond words. Your support means the world to me now and then when times were hard, it was good to know that someone cared.

Again, I appreciate all whom I served with and with sincere thanks, I bid you all farewell and God Bless You All

Words From the Author

It is with great pleasure that I share with you many of my hands on experiences dealt with in the United States Army. This is a story about one of the greatest organizations in the world, yet rooted within this are many struggles. It offers comfort to some knowing that someone else has been where he or she is now. It offers understanding to others who have had many questions over the years. To others it will be painful to read, for it might cause them to relive their struggles over again as they read the story. It will make some people angry and others happy. Some will strongly disagree with some of the statements and allegations made about this great organization. Others will say this is just a "Black Man" trying to make a name for himself. It must be understood that I am proud to be a Black Man and would never want to be anything else color wise. The ultimate goal that I wanted to achieve during my military career was to be accepted as a Man that just happen to be a Black Man. As you read this book you will have a chance for yourself to see if I accomplished that goal.

Finally, this book will do what it was generated to do in the end: **Enlighten all on the fact that no matter how much you want to think that racism; discrimination, favoritism, and other distractions that hinder a "Total Freedom" for All to excel does not exist, it does**. Everyday someone is attacked just because of the color of his or her skin. Everyday someone is attacked because of what they believe. Everyday someone is attacked because they fail to conform to what Organizations, Leaderships or Private Companies desire because of selfish reasons. Could this be you now in the midst of your endeavor as Man or Woman who only desires to be accepted as the Man or Woman you are?

To the **Civilian World** I encourage to read this book about one of the greatest organizations that has issues dealing with racism, discrimination, favoritism and a host of other controversial issues that you deal with on a daily basis. **Knowledge is the beginning of Wisdom and from there you get what this book ultimately brings UNDERSTANDING.** Through my dealings with the outside civilian world over the past 3 years, it has elevated my level of understanding tremendously. **The issues out here are even more controversial than many of those I faced in the United States Army, yet the root of them are the same. This story will enrich your life with the knowledge, wisdom and understanding of the events that go unnoticed by many civilians during their daily walk of life.**

So in closing, know that whatever your response is to this book and its contents: I am a "Man" that others will continue to only see as a "Black Man"

PRELUDE

The walk down the road of life that I was about to embark on would be a strange one in many ways. It was intriguing to know that a Man was about to make his mark on the United States Army. It was a moment in time when you could see it all coming. The young Man from the heart of the country was ready and poised to enter the big world and see what he could achieve in it. I was not afraid, yet the bubbles within me were bubbling. I was excited and yearning more than ever to embark on this journey. During the months leading up to my entry, I pondered how it would be to walk a mile in the shoes of soldiers. I had never fired a weapon, yet I knew there was a strong possibility that I would have to one day. The thought of death was the ultimate thing that made this journey full of expectations. The matter of war was all around in the news. To say that the fear of death made me have second thoughts would be an understatement. I just pictured myself standing on the battlefield facing the enemy. The thought of firing upon the enemy caused goose bumps rise within me. The day was approaching and I began to see the dynasty beginning. I was pumped on the inside and it was time to go off to the United States Army. The ride on the bus clearly had my attention. I was leaving home and did not know if I would be returning. The United States Army was about to be my home. The comfort of the bed at home was almost over. I would no longer have the comfort of having a mother and father to provide for me anymore. The fear began to set in and I still knew within that there was no turning back.

I entered the Recruiting Station with nothing but expectations. I had no clue what was going to happen. Yet, I knew it was a part of my destiny to be where I was then. It was a pleasant feeling to be away from home. I had always dreamed of being on my own as an adult. I wanted to experience what it was like to provide for myself. The most rewarding thing that I thought I would experience was the power of being able to do what I wanted, when I wanted. It all was falling into place. Then something happened, I was sworn into Active Duty. After the ceremony, everything changed. The pleasant attitudes seemed to all disappear. The voices all became command voices. **You are a soldier now, get in a hurry.** I really began to have fear and this was only the beginning. It would be a stay filled with many twists and turns. ***I would have to deal with discrimination, racism and many attempts of personal vengeance.*** There would be many attacks to take away the dream and vision of Retiring from this great organization. My patience and ability to stick to my inner convictions would be tested to the core of all I stood for from within. There would be many controversial days not knowing whether I would survive the many schemes that would come my way. ***The barriers that I would have to cross would be many. Being that I was a Black Man would proved to be the greatest barrier at times.*** The road to the vision shown to me of my military career would come with a great cost. It would almost cost me all I had: My Life. The nights were dark and days were long, as I awaited answers of my status within the United States Army.

INTRODUCTION

The time has come for me to share with the world my story of the United States Army. **The story is full of alarming experiences that show the struggles of a young black soldier as he tried to make his mark in the United States Army**. One of the greatest things that you could ever do in life is put your life on the line for your country. It enables you to contribute the protection of freedom. The sacrifice made on a daily basis is unbelievable. The price you pay for this arduous task is insurmountable. The pride that you serve with shows how much you have on the inside to preserve freedom. **Freedom to me was very important because in times past, our freedom was limited as a black race. To find myself in the midst of the preservation of the very freedom my ancestors could not enjoy was very emotional.** The inner feelings that drove my emotion were moving at a high level of intensity. I had no clue as to what I was getting myself involved with. I knew death was at the center point of what the United States Army was calling me to do. I did have fears within, but the thoughts of what was to come were intense. I spent many days speculating on how my life would change after Active Duty.

Joining the Armed Forces in the year of **1980** was one of the greatest life-changing events. I have an adventure that contains many great moments, obstacles and hurdles I jumped over. As a boy coming from the country, I was entering a completely different world. I clearly understood the road from the beginning would not be an easy one. The rides on the bus to **Jacksonville, Florida** gave me many hours to reflect on where I was heading. I entered the recruiting station with the intention of embarking on the journey of my life to date. Coming from the country life was in many ways to my advantage. Working hard was not a problem for me in that I grew up on a farm, and it gave me hard working ethics. I needed a change of scenery along with the desire to expand my knowledge and wisdom of the wide-based world. I knew it would be a challenge to deal with people from all over the world. I had many questions and doubts about what I was about to embark on. Despite all the questions and doubts about what to expect, there was never a hesitation about not embarking on the quest. There were times in this story that depression was at a high level. The time period of a twenty years plus campaign within the Armed Forces was full of joy, sadness, shock and many other emotions that brought out the complexity of the attacks the United States Army would bring upon me.

I have chosen over the past twenty years to pay the price for being that I am me! I have continuously faced adversity for making that choice. The result of it all has been many pains and heartaches. I always felt that accomplishment of the mission and the welfare of all soldiers was the utmost reason I was placed in the elite Non-Commissioned Officers' Corp. I love the United States Army and would not give up the past twenty years for anything this world could offer me. These past twenty years, coupled with the rearing that I received growing up has made me the solid human being that I am today. I know that it sounds conceited at times, but the results achieved during these past twenty years speak for themselves. The one test of life is how strong you are when the odds are against you. When everything around you is crumbling down, what do you do when it may be no relief in sight? Faith is a powerful word and that is the one word that allowed me to stand here today. I have not always been a smart soldier my entire career. At times, I proved to be my own worst enemy. Doing the right thing was not always the most important thing for the question of " Are you the one to do the right thing? Battles in this life are not always ours to fight. That was a hard lesson for me to learn. That leads back to what was the vision that I received from the Lord concerning my military career. He showed me a glimpse of the end: that I would retire after twenty years as an E-7." What he did not show me were the fights and battles that would confront me during those years. In the fulfillment of that vision, there would be many of them. The vision I was shown was ironic in that it would be the only thing I had to hold on to at times during the past twenty years. It was a great source of comfort when the light looked dim and on the way to blowing out.

There is nothing in this world that could compare to having all around you see the odds standing against you. The story starts in **Jacksonville, Florida** at the reception station where a young man was looking for a new home. I had to endure many setbacks in the road to making my mark on the awesome organization. I never knew that on July 23, 1980 when I entered active duty that I would have to endure such a twisted road to complete the vision and the dream received from the Lord about my military career. I went on to find myself at **Fort Knox, Kentucky** where Basic Training would start to change my life forever. It was there where I first encountered controversy, while maturing as a soldier and a young man. At times I felt like calling it quits, yet my inner self would not allow it to happen. To my surprise, it was soon over and I was a Basic Training Graduate. With a bus ride on the road, I ventured to **Fort Benjamin Harrison, Indiana** to complete Advanced Individual Training. It was here where I begin to see the United States Army in another light. For some unknown reason all the rules had changed and nothing was the same anymore. Some eight weeks later I was a graduate of the Personnel Administration Specialist Course. This graduation brought to pass the first two obstacles of becoming a soldier. After four months of intense training, I was finally a qualified soldier.

This started me on the journey that would change my life even more. A journey that would take me to the foreign land of **Germany.** There I endured many depressing moments, yet there were many positives that brought me moments of joy. The home of the roughriders was where I was given a solid foundation to build on. Death was certain if war started yet the beauty of the country made this tour of duty bearable. I had more questions than answers about how the United States Army functioned. Yet when it was all said and done, I had a successful tour that led me to a leadership role. Here I was a young twenty-year old man expected to lead soldiers into battle.

The journey would further lead to the land of **Fort Huachuca, Arizona**, The lesson learned during this time would definitely prove to be deadly at one point. The massive amount of hostility that surfaced during this tour of duty would force my maturity level to greatly increase. Things would happen outside the realm of the United States Army that would also alter my life, as I knew it forever. Could there be wedding bells in the air? Here again, time would pass and bring this tour of duty to a conclusion. Upon the completion of this tour, the stakes were much higher and the tension had been drawn between the good and evil forces within the United States Army. The question was who would prevail in the end?

In the air again, heading to the foreign land of **Germany** for the second time. This time around would prove to be more hostile than any tour of duty to date. The forces of evil were rearing their heads from all directions and there seemed to be no relief in sight. For the first time, I fought racism head to head and the battle to do right was forever facing me through it all. **The amazing thing about this racism and discrimination is that it was blatant and performed in the open. All parties involved made it known through their actions that it really did not matter that I knew about it. I lived with those blatant acts of racism for over 16 months with no relief in sight as I knew relief to be.** Through all of the adversities faced at this tour of duty, I was still standing in the end. I had control and a distraught mind all at once. Yet when it was all done another feather had been added to the completion of the vision and the dream. As I prepared to leave this tour of duty, I realized that my tenacity and forcefulness as a soldier had taken a form of an attitude. I would not be denied anymore. I knew the fight was going to be raised to another level of intensity as I departed the foreign land of Germany for the last time.

It was that inner mentality that boarded the plane en route to land of the Airborne, **Fort Bragg, North Carolina.** After some 8 years of quality service, how could I have known about the massive amount of jealousy, envy and malicious schemes that would be thrown my way? The negative side of the United States Army had reared its ugly head. It was here I had to face the fight of my life. The vicious attacks that came with these 6 years proved to be fatal to my military career at times. **All that I had to depend on during the almost fatal attack on my dream and vision was FAITH.** That faith in the vision and the dream increased greatly after some 11 and a half years of service, when it was tested to the maximum level. The fight was fierce and arduous in intensity. Sleepless nights were full of my daily walk of life within this command. I had an enormous amount of pressure on me all six years of this arduous duty. Here it was some 6 years that had passed and I survived the many deceptive schemes.

I was headed for my new duty station with many scars and open wounds. What a drive it was to the land of **Fort Lewis Washington**. Shortly after my arrival to this tour of duty, I was selected to promotion at the final stage of the vision and the dream. Who would have thought this would start the war games all over again. Despite the fact that all the schemes were the same, I was not the same. Over the past 14 years, I had grown from a young black soldier into a mature man that was a force to be reckoned with. Here I was a seasoned soldier with a wealth of knowledge, wisdom and understanding. All the turmoil through the years had brought me to such a time as this. Within a 2-½ year period, I had been a part of 4 organizations. There was reviews, relief of cause, complaints filed and to top it all off a promotion. The assaults during this time could and would have been fatal for the average soldier. Yet when it was all over the United States Army knew that the young man from the country had grown up to be a stable force in the United States Army.

The tour was over and I was headed toward a hardship tour in **Korea.** The maturity of which I was would come forth like never before. The end was near and that within itself was the key to my desire to mature and learn like never before. I was allowed a status where I could make a difference with positive results. The schemes were still in affect, but one by one I met them head on. Soon the roughest tour of duty of my life would soon be over. I returned to the homeland of the United States.

Here, it was that headed to the air assault territory **Fort Campbell, Kentucky**. This duty station would prove to be the place where it would all come together. All that I had endured in the past 18 years would come full circle during this tour of duty. Who would have thought that a country boy from the small town of Monticello, Florida would have to endure such an awesome and tremendous tour of duty in the United States Army? Now get ready for the rest of the story: The United States Army from the Eyes of a **"Man"**, who's others, saw only as a **"Black Man"**. It was a positive in my life for it increased my already strong faith. I know without any doubt that I am one of God's Chosen Vessels. I seek no retribution for anyone over this matter, for I know that all involved will reap what he or she sows.

This story is a farewell to the greatest organization within the United States Army, the Non-Commissioned Officers. Many questions about racism, discrimination, equal opportunity and a fair playing field for all that serve will be answered within this book. Controversial could be the one word to describe the career the young man from the heart of the country. The 20 years of service rendered to this United State's Army has been rewarding, yet it has left some tremendous scars that will always be there to remind me that:

"Whatever you do, it is going to cost you. Are you willing to pay the price?"

CHAPTER I

THE FOUNDATION: MY CHILDHOOD

I was one of nine children and I was the second oldest. We were raised in the country where the nearest store was 20-30 minutes away by car. I do not remember my early five years of life, but I can remember 1968 when the death of Martin Luther King, Jr., along with all the noise made about Black people being allowed to vote. During the next six years of my life, nothing major happened until I was twelve years old and accepted Jesus Christ as my personal savior. Also, at that age, my oldest brother left for the United States Army and left me in charge of seven brothers and sisters. The next six years would be full of me growing up through many adversities that made me stronger in knowledge and wisdom. I went through the entire school year with five pairs of pants and six shirts, none of them were new. I never got to participate in any activities at the school because of my responsibilities at home. I worked from the age of fourteen and all money was given to my parents to support the household. During my childhood I experienced many of the survival tools that others my age know nothing about. The following was the source of my childhood and propelled me today where I am: Outhouse, Washtubs, Rubboards, Clotheslines, Turn Plows, Purple Hulls, Black Eyed Peas, Butter Beans, Sweet Potatoes, Watermelons, Corn, Hogs, Chickens, and many other country living resources.

Outhouse was where I spent many quality spiritual hours with God. During the entire 18 years of my childhood, we never had an inside toilet. It was that which caused me to build up such a strong faith in God. We had learned how to hold our bowel movements until daylight came because of not having the luxury of a toilet being on the inside. I believe that we were the only family that used the outside toilet in our community. I cannot count the many times that I had to clean that outhouse and fertilize the cane field behind it. I managed to get the courage to endure many night hours within this outhouse and thus leading to a powerful praise relationship with God. I needed his protection from any harm from down below and that was the source of my praise to God for protection.

Washtubs/Rubboards was another part of my life for 18 years. The means of having our clothes cleaned was through many hours of rubbing back and forth. Clothes lines were always awaiting me to hang out the clothes that had just went through the outdoor cleaning procedure. Washing machines and dryers was something that I never experienced during my childhood. One washtub with wash water and another washtub with rinse made what I now call the hand operated washing machine with two cycles: wash and rinse. Up and down the rubboard was a daily routine in my life during my childhood. Between the farming and all the other challenges I faced on a daily basis, you could believe how getting into my own world washing clothes up and down the rubbing board was a relief from it all

School was where I performed many of the devious things during my childhood. It was during these times that I would make a mark that led many teachers to believe that my future was not too bright. The effort made during class was one of being the class clown and no effort was ever made to obtain the maximum potential that was within me academically. I did just enough to get grades that would keep me out of trouble at home. I can remember on many occasions when I came short of the mark and felt the wrath for not doing the best I could in school. The thought of attending any college was never a part of my academic walk of life. It was all about having fun and somehow making grades to stay out of trouble. During the grades of Kindergarten through the 9th grade I just coasted with mediocre grades and managed to clown to the point that I never got in any trouble at school that my parents had to be informed about. Then came the 10th grade and that is where life for me in school begins to take a course that proved to be very unpleasant for me. It was one day when I was headed for the bus and turned to one of my teachers and said words that I knew would cause me the ultimate embarrassment to the whole community in which I was such a visible part of. I knew that those words would cost me more than all the other bad things I done in school thus far. I made sure I wore the best outfit I had for school the next day and it was that outfit that took me into the principal's office. Hoping that he would give me three of the powerful paddling licks was not to be this time. He levied me with a 3-day suspension. I had reached an all time low and the worst thing that could have happened to me, happened. The nice young man of the community had just been exposed to be who he really was a failure. I did not know what to do, yet I knew this would prove to change my whole life in one way or the other. I had the three horrible days to deal with as the first kid of the household to get suspended from school. There was something else that I had to deal with that was far worst than the fact that I was suspended from school, it was the fact that I had went beyond the rules established in the "Respect Your Elder Arena". The 16-year-old "Quiet Kid" had just been exposed and to make matters worse nobody wanted to talk about it, to include my parents. I needed someone to help me and for the first time the beating did not come so freely and this made me feel worst. Who would have ever thought that not getting a beating would make me upset. I needed to be released and that was no where in sight from those who I knew loved me. For the first time I had a situation that I had to handle alone. After many hours of meditation, I got the relief I was seeking: The suspension from school was a wakeup call for me to start being who I was and stop the role playing at home and away from home. It was at that point that I went through a life transformation that would affect the rest of my life. The truth realized was " I had not let down the community, school, or any others involved, it was myself who was the beneficiary of this failure. All things as I knew them in my life changed from that moment and I saw life in a different light from then on.

Church was the one place that gave me a sacred place to release the grueling issues I had to deal with during my childhood. This is the on area where I experienced very hardtimes during the 6-year period after accepting Jesus Christ as my personal savior in the year of 1975. You see I was one of those people who loved to sing praises to God during my early days of childhood. I would sing those praises in the woods and most of all in the **Outhouse**. We were brought in a state of participating in all the holiday programs at the churches by at a minimum saying a speech or participating in a play. One of the most dramatic events during those early days was when I was asked to sing a solo on one of the programs. I was quiet during that period of time, yet singing for God was something that brought boldness out of me. The song was "Come to Jesus" and that song would prove to change my church life forever. After that song, I got a message from my father: "you will have to get some religion and until then you will not sing anymore songs in the church". This news proved to be devastating to me at first and somewhat confusing. Here it was that we had been made to participate in all these programs and now it was being taken away. By that time I had grown to love church and I was not going to allow this to stop me. During the upcoming revival at our church I started out to seek that religion. It all started during the first week of 1975 in the month of August. It would be some 13 days later and I had not found that religion. Time was running out on me and I was growing frustrated because I knew I had received him as savior, but I could not bring myself to proclaim it out of my mouth. Then there came Saturday night and I walked to the church for what could have been the last chance during that year of revival. I got to the church and saw that the hour had come and gone and proceeded to go back home. There came the family that I have grown to love even until this day that turned me around from making the biggest mistake of my life. The devil had played on my disappointment and led me to believe that all had given up on me ever confessing Jesus Christ as my savior. I did not confess on that night, but I did that very next morning and thus started the greatest roller coaster of my life. During the next 6 years I had many good times and yet in the midst of them I had many difficult moments that forced me to grow up spiritually fast. There were many Sunday School Conventions and some Church Conventions that I attended. There were many lining of Hymns and Prayers that were given throughout the community as we traveled. In the midst of all that were the many adversities that I faced daily: Feeling that the task of living right was not achieved and having the burden of drawing the rest of the community into a personal relationship with Jesus Christ through my life lived daily. I contemplated death at times because those two goals were never met as I saw and read what it took to complete it. I felt that I lost my whole childhood trying to live for God, yet I knew within it was the right thing to do. It would not be until some 20 years after accepting Jesus Christ as my savior that I got the understanding that I had been searching for all those years. The stage had been set spiritually for me to see if the training received would be able to propel me to the completion of the Dream and Vision received from God about my tour of duty within the United States Army.

Mother was a great source of teaching me about doing the right things in life. I cannot count the many times that I heard encouraging words from my mother as she taught me to do the right things in life. I must admit that many times I did not heed to her words and there was a price to pay at the end of the day when my father arrived home. She taught me the values of knowing how to do the little things in life such as cooking, cleaning and most of all facing all challenges that life brought my way. The memory of one occasion was when she told me not to ride the neighbors' bicycle while on the way to pick okra at one of summer work areas. Feeling that I could do it and get away with proved to be a mistake. After getting on the bicycle halfway to the house, I had what some would call an accident. I was all skinned up and that was not the worst of it all. I lost half a tooth and would you believe it was one of those in the front. I had to live with that tooth being out in the front for some 2 plus years. It served as a reminder that when you are disobedient to those who have rule over you, the consequences can be dramatically negative. It was those things that my mother was good at and over time I grew to understand that disobedient would cost you in ways you never imagined. The broken tooth changed the way I talked and served as constant reminder that I rode a bicycle that I was admonished not to ride. Thanks to Mother, I had teachings that have stuck with me even until this day.

Father was the enforcer of whether or not I did the right thing while growing up in his house. Many times I broke the rules and paid dearly. He worked very hard to have us taken care of with the necessities of life. I knew that some things could be counted on no matter how hard things got: a place to sleep and food to eat. During these years there were many times when I had no clue or appreciation for the rearing I was receiving. I was in the selfish mode and was only thinking about myself and many times made foolish statements about gladly leaving when I became 18 years old. In retrospect I did not know how blessed I was and since leaving home I have grown to know that all the hardtimes experienced during my childhood is the very reason why I am where I am today some 24 years later. During all those times during my childhood when I felt my Father was unfair, I now see that all the time he could see further than I could see as a child. His stern hands of discipline enabled me to be the disciplined adult that I am today and had a profound affect of the story you are about to hear about my walk within the United States Army.

In the end, I learned to love both my parents for the role they played in my life enabling me to be ready to handle the world and my quest in the year of 1980 in the United States Army. During the past 24 years after my grueling childhood, I started to see all the reasons why my parents raised me the way they did. There is value in training up a child in the way he should go and it will not depart him. I am a living witness that it was that training that propelled me to the high level of achievements during my adult years after what I labeled as: The foundation-my Childhood. **Finally**, I left home in 1980 with a dream and a vision: That I would do 20 years in the United States Army and make a difference in the world first as a Man and secondly as a Black Man. You see Black men have been marked for years by the world. The odds were against me from the start, but I was determined to achieve my goals through all I had been through over the past eighteen years: FAITH IN GOD!

CHAPTER II

A YOUNG BLACK MAN ENTERS BASIC TRAINING

A YOUNG BLACK MAN entered the United States Army to make his mark in the Armed Forces. I saw a great opportunity to serve my country and see the world. My inspirations were high as I prepared to go off on a life-changing adventure. To find myself serving my country twelve years after we as Black Americans had received the right to vote was awesome in many ways. The first thing that went through my mind was what rights would I have as a Black soldier? I knew that it would be beyond expectation not to encounter any racism and discrimination from people within the military. I was full of emotions in that I had no clue about what I was getting into. I knew that when it was over, it would be history in the making. I had all kinds of thoughts about adversities that I would encounter. The Basic Training encounters that I faced were **A New Way of Life**; different type of authority, variety of personalities expected to jell and function as a team. I had to adjust really fast to what I called the **'More Advanced World'**. Mother and Father were no longer there to protect their son. I had to face many consequences for my actions. I had to dig deep within my inner self and find the motivation to hang in there. The atmosphere was forever changing and that made my adjustments come quicker. The authorities were all different. At home, I knew and understood the players.

The first day of active duty was totally opposite of the Recruiting Station experience in that the intensity increased. The need to be responsible was incredible. I found myself wondering about what a road I have chosen. They sent me from the Recruiting Station with the task of ensuring that ten to fifteen other soldiers arrived at our destination of Fort Knox, Kentucky. The bus ride was a thoughtful one for me, in that the fear of the unknown was traveling within my mind. Upon our arrival at **Fort Knox, KY** we met some men that instilled the fear of God within us even more. We had to put the duffel bags on our backs and marched about one-mile. The noise that we heard during the march was fierce. The first two days were forever putting us through changes. We lost our civilian clothes to the cellar. The trip to the barbershop was an enlightening one. They asked us how we wanted our hair cut, to only see our hair hit the floor. The mirror told us that we did not belong to ourselves anymore. The fact that we belonged to the United States Army was beginning to sink in. I really had a lot to think about then. I had more unresolved questions than I had solutions. The one thing that amazed me was the ability I displayed in adapting to the many changes I faced daily. The Drill Sergeants were interesting. We had three of them. They all had their own personality and rules. The first words that became a part of our daily lives were, **"Drill Sergeant coming, make a hole! "** Those words strongly implied get out of the way. I viewed **Phase One** of basic training as: **"A Stage of Adjusting to a New Way of Life"**. The relationship that I had with my Drill Sergeants was strange. It seemed that they constantly told me to dig holes and place

cigarette butts in them. I made it known, during several Police Calls, that I did not pick up butts because I did not smoke them.
The Drill Sergeant hearing this found a tool to use against me when I frustrated him. I cannot remember the number of times that I found myself digging a hole. While digging a number of holes, I found out that keeping my mouth shut would save me a whole lot of grief. I quickly found out that to complain was not the approach to take. I then formed the rule that a "smile" would replace the complaining. This would grow to become my expression for the many dilemmas in which I would find myself. After the first three weeks, the training intensified and so did the mind games that I labeled as distractions. The fight for Best-Platoon was in full force. I found myself in the best platoon and that made the other Drill Sergeants target us to see if we would break under pressure. Here in Basic Training, it was all learned day by day. Each situation seemed to bring out something new from our Drill Sergeants. Looking for someone to talk to about the next move was unavailable at times. For once in my life, I had to make my own decisions. I was not an expert and the consequences that I had to face caused me to give deep thought about what to do next time I faced the same dilemma. The action was happening fast for me and there were times that I wanted to quit. The times when I was doing the low crawl, eating dirt, with a Drill Sergeant saying, "Get down and crawl!" Others times, I faced one of my many confrontations with my Drill Sergeants. I guess you could say I had a problem with submitting to authority. That is what went through the heads of leaders as they dealt with the young man from Monticello, Florida. The events were strange, but many strange things were happening within that Basic Training Camp. On one occasion, I was taken in the bathroom and offered an opportunity to take a swipe at the Drill Sergeant. Deep inside, I was asking if this was real. I told him I just wanted to complete Basic Training. He retreated and put his Drill hat back on. I wondered many days afterward what I had done to bring that on. The results that were coming my way caused me to change my philosophy of life. Maturity was coming quickly in many ways. I was enduring changes rapidly. Another occasion, I managed to drop my weapon while on a Ruck march. That was one of the most out of Army character things to do. I spent my whole break holding my weapon over my head. With a Drill Sergeant breathing down a lecture to me. I had grown to the point where I said few words. I just smiled and this irritated the Drill Sergeant to death. I had learned that opening my mouth only led to push-ups and burying cigarette butts in the dirt. I needed to learn how to make my mark on the United States Army with many adversities facing me daily. Mouthing off would prove to be wrong at this time. How great was this part of the experience to me, in that it was making a solid man of me in a short period of time.

Life was full of smaller agonizing moments during these days of Basic Training. Many times I developed what some would call an attitude. The fact that I seemed to have a negative attitude was far from the truth. I just wanted to survive because I knew that I could not go home as a failure. The other driving factor was that home, for me, was now the United States Army and the desire to go home was non-existent.

I made it clear that when I left home, I left home. There was no turning back. I was in the United States Army for the long haul and no matter what I had to endure at that home, I would find a way to prevail. Evidence of that was when I found myself qualifying with a patch over my eye. To this day I cannot say I really hit those targets. The longest episode was when I was out at the **Qualification Range.** I had never fired a weapon in my life and did not have a clue to what I was doing. I had all kinds of complications in trying to get qualified. I found myself trying to figure out which side I shot from. After figuring that out, I had a major problem. I could not close my eye to see the targets. The Drill Sergeant was getting highly upset, because some way or the other I had to get qualified. I started weaving the field and that led to many thoughts. This was not laughing matter to me and with almost everybody qualified and I'm struggling, was not funny. After many attempts to work it out, I finally qualified. Often placing a patch over my eye seemed absurd but I was determined to prevail when it was all over. Again, I cannot honestly say I hit any of the targets, but I knew the dirt popped up. Thank God, this ordeal was over and was one of the roughest times I had during Basic Training. The frustration of this long day stayed with me for a while. I would hear about it from time to time from the Drill Sergeants.

The Physical Training of Basic Training at Fort Knox, Kentucky was very interesting. We found ourselves in the midst of all kinds of uniforms. We even found ourselves running in Combat boots. I was young and always did my best to hang in there with all they did. It was hot and that did not help in anyway at all. The sweat came down, drenching a many days as we performed the Physical Training for the day. It was the middle of the summer and survival was the key to daily performance of duty. I was set on getting through this tedious ordeal and would not allow anything to deter the goal we all desired: Completion of Basic Training. Another episode, which proved to be the most embarrassing moment of my life, was when we had an inspection by my Superior Officer. It must be understood that during this term of Basic Training this was my first introduction to the United States Army Officer Corp. Thus far it was mind-boggling, because of the fact all the officers I had saw seemed to be of the same race. Despite being a young man, it was the structure of the United States Army. I did ponder the issue too much, being that it was about race. To keep hearing my race always saying, "Yes, sir!" to the white race regardless of age bothered me. Here I was in the presence of them that had sent my race into a constant set of submissive actions. I had not experienced any racism to date, but it was impossible to forget these hard times of the past eighteen years. My parents had endured many rough times that caused me so much pain. I had always promised myself that when I got out in the world, things would be different. I always had been trained to respect my elders regardless of their race. The ultimate act in Basic Training was when we were getting ready for the Superior Officer to walk through the barracks. The Drill Sergeants were walking through trying to prepare us, new recruits for the walkthrough. While waiting, I felt I would have no problem when he arrived. The word attention recruits sounded that signified he was in the barracks. I had never seen an officer that close in the flesh since I had been on active duty. I was poised and thought I was ready. It proved to be very different seeing them from afar, than having one about to come face to face with me. As he moved down the line, I started to change. Here I was about to be confronted by an officer who happened to be a white man. It seemed that all the acts of submission that I had seen in my childhood were going through my head. I still felt within that moment I would be able to handle it all when he was in front of me. The time arrived and he stood and began to speak to me. I heard him ask what my name was and here came the most embarrassing moment of my life: I could not tell him what my name was. I cannot say what else was said, but when he left me I was very disappointed in myself. The effects of the childhood experiences were strong and for the first time I had to face it. I fell short of the promise I had made. It seemed fear had overcome me in that moment. The inner feelings were all disappointing and negative. I was very angry at my performance during the moment of truth.

I went to bed that night in deep thought and that morning I had a change of attitude: As long as I lived and served in the United States Army, I would never be afraid of any man again. They put their pants on one leg at a time like I did, and there was no need to be afraid. This incident would prove to be the foundation of my awesome military career. I knew that I was out there with the big boys and I had to grow up fast if I was going to survive. Survival was the key function during my early days in the United States Army. I had managed to maintain it this far. What the future would hold for me depended upon how I adjusted to the many changes I encountered daily. The ability to work was instilled within me, but this world was totally new. So the upcoming days would be a challenge and I was doubtful if I was ready after the most embarrassing moment of my life had just occurred. Learning from the various experiences was vital, because doing them over and over again would prove to be painful. It was the Five Event Exercise Physical Fitness Test that was tough during my Basic Training. It consisted of handlebars, Run, Dodge, and Jump, Inverted Crawl, Low Crawl, and the <u>fifth</u> event. These events had a lot of strain and stress on certain parts of the body. It seemed as though every time our platoon went to chow, we either did the handlebars or the Low Crawl. It was during the Low Crawl that I scratched my elbows and decided that I had enough of this lunch time physical training. I went to Sick Call and got put on a three-day profile. After coming back, I felt weird about the whole thing. I knew within myself it was not the pain that battered me, it was the *idea of doing what I was before going to eat. I felt deep within myself that for the first* time I had wimped out. That did not make me feel good on the inside. I had finally let the Basic Training get the best of me. I knew that I could not do anything about that part, but it would not happen again. My frame of mind began to change and there was no doubt that I was going to the graduation ceremony. I had heard many negatives over the past few weeks, but all of them together did not have the effect the Sick Call incident had. I was changing and no one knew it but me. I had a new way of looking at the military as a whole. Physical Training became better and the drive to call a few cadences was aroused within and signs of little abilities within surprised me.

PHASE TWO OF BASIC TRAINING was more enlightening in that it started to introduce us to the relaxing part of the military. The Copper Club was a hangout for the Bravo Fifteen-Four Battalion. There we began to have fun and learn what it was like to meet other soldiers. The bond that we had formed during the first few weeks made us a close-knit team of soldiers trying to uphold the Battalion's honor. Within our platoon, we had various feelings about each other. Some were good and others were not. The amazing thing that I had found within me was the ability to decide and do what I felt to be right. The peer pressure was high, yet I was my own person. The determination within itself would drive me during my time I had to make changes in doing the right thing as led. Leadership was beginning to come alive as we found ourselves traveling outside of the battalion's area. We all had to ensure that all were taken care of and that would lead to finding out what leaders were within the group. How amazing it was to discover that during these rough times, I would move to the forefront and make decisions that I never knew were within me to make. The road marches were stressful and all the **roads** were interesting. The road marches were done and proved to be one of the most strenuous parts of Basic Training. We had a lot of practice of marching from place to place. Yet when you add a **rucksack, weapon** and other equipment, you took the level of durability up to levels beyond most of our imaginations. I remember the first one that I went on and it took all within me to finish it. The fact that I had flat feet did not help me at all. The pain I endured was tremendous, yet the desire to make it to the finish line was the overbearing factor to my success. After that initiation to what the United States Army called a road march, I knew what to expect during the future ones. The affect of these marches took its told on the Drill Sergeants also, they had to walk each mile with us and that showed for the first times some of their weakness. The reality of it all was that age played a role in how much the body could take on a daily basis. During these marches, I saw first hand what I would have to face in my upcoming days in the United States Army. Over the next few weeks, we would go on two to three such marches. They would come through rain, winds and other obstacles, but in the end we all met the requirements of succeeding in the United States Army road marches.

As we entered the mature last two weeks of Basic Training, I was riding on High Street within. There was a powerful sense of a great accomplishment as the graduation date approached. I was laughing and smiling more than ever. Still aggravated at a couple of the Drill Sergeants, yet that was not the focal point of my actions. I was looking forward to the day when the young Man from **Monticello, Florida** would be a graduate from Basic Training. Five weeks of strenuous training had forced me to grow up in many ways. The maturity was there, despite the fact that it was not well groomed. I started to believe that I could be a soldier after all. Most of training was over; all that remained for me was to stay out of trouble. That was not a

problem for me. It seemed like the days grew longer and the pressure was mounting against us. The top Drill Sergeant could see that we were beginning to sink under the pressure. He came in and gave us an intensified lecture. It started with the throwing of a trash can down the hallway. He informed us of the fact that we were better than the mind games that the other Drill Sergeants were playing. He told us that working together and taking care of each other would be the key to us maintaining the **Top Platoon Status.** It was then that I had to replay the most embarrassing moment in my life again, saying it again and learning from it again.
What is your name? ". I could not say what my name was. To lose the knowledge of what my name was gave me a totally new perspective on life. I must say that the effect of that moment was never so important and life altering as it was at this point. It was during my off time when my ability to lead came alive. There were many confrontations between soldiers from other units. Many fights occurred. The fact that we were a team made us become one another's keeper. It did not matter whether or not we liked each other, we knew that whatever went down would affect us all. Knowing that made us our brother/soldier keepers. The sense of confidence that I displayed when we were out from the barracks was overwhelming. We did our share of fighting within the barracks, but outside, we were a strong force to be reckoned with. The whole key to survival was talk, but ensure no incident happened. The calmness of this platoon showed the most when we were under pressure.

I was not the designated leader, but I had many words when it came down to leaving a potential dangerous situation. Life in Basic Training had grown to be a family affair. People all over the world had come together at Fort Knox. Kentucky and became a close-knit family. Color did not matter at this stage. We were all in this for survival. There was tension between some of us, but the thought of being locked in the barracks kept the tempers down. Peer pressure was at a high velocity within my platoon. We believed in making sure the one messing up knew it and got it together. Most of my encounters did not have an affect on the platoon's fate, but it had an affect on me. I was not the best soldier you could want, but I knew that was a phase for me. Graduation Day was fast approaching and things began to lighten up for the training was over. Here I go, about to graduate Basic Training and move to Fort Benjamin Harrison, Indiana Advanced Individual Training. The Drill Sergeant was saying many things but at that point in time, it did not matter. I was used to being the underdog when it came down to success. The one thing I knew was that I, as a Man, would soon be a graduate of Basic Training. That could not be taken away from me no matter what. Within my inner being, I was marveling at the accomplishment. It would be the start to a long and exciting military career. To think that it all started in Fort Knox, Kentucky. What an awesome accomplishment. The day finally arrived for us to graduate from a vigorous Basic Training. The breakup of the team was very sentimental, needless to say, full of tears. The final departing words occurred with my Drill Sergeant as we boarded the bus for **Fort Benjamin Harrison, IN.** He informed the soldiers with me to take care of me. He implied that my future within the United

States Army was limited. Thus ends my basic training ride within the military.
Tears were shed as we departed each other. The bars of support were being broken and we all knew that an even greater challenge awaited us. The first half of the equation was complete. Now, only Advanced Individual Training stood in the way of becoming a soldier. Let the screams come from the mountaintop, for here comes the Man from Monticello, Florida to the state of Indiana.

Basic Training was nice while it lasted, but now I must move on. Good bye, never will I forget the actions of the last seven weeks. Wow!!!

CHAPTER III

THE JOURNEY BEGINS: GERMANY

THE ROAD to Germany was a lonely and scary one. There were many fears bottled up inside of me, yet there was a little feeling of excitement driving me to know that I was in for a adventure filled experience. Upon my arrival to Germany, I was processed and introduced to the rail system, German style. I was told going to sleep would be dangerous. For sleep could give soldiers a tour of the whole country. The instructions were when you hear Wurzburg, Germany, move quickly. The ride gave me a chance to see the people of Germany first hand. I saw many strange things that would lead me to believe this would be an adventurous tour. I listened at every stop for my signal to get off. This was a fast moving train and alertness was the key to success. I got there OK and proceeded on to in process at the Headquarters of the Division where I would be assigned. It would be over the next few days that I would get acclimated to the New Command and its philosophy. I knew I was heading to the Land of the Roughriders, as I called them. One memorable event that occurred during this stay happened while I was standing in line to eat breakfast: I was standing behind a Sergeant in line, and I spoke to him with words to this affect: "Good morning, how are you doing Sergeant?" The reply made to me was an eye opener to what the United States Army was about. He said, "I'm doing fine, how are you doing, Private?" This little statement that seemed harmless, would have an adverse affect on me for my entire stay in the United States Army. Just in that moment, I seemed so belittled, yet it went deeper than that. All the memories of my growing up days flashed before me in an instance. At that very moment, racism pondered through my mind, as it had never done before. Being that the words came from a Caucasian, made it all the more real. At first there was fear, and then a calm came over me all of a sudden. I found comfort in knowing that the United States Army would dare to let racism become an issue in this day and time. Despite that calmness, I had questions in the back of my mind that I knew would be answered in the upcoming years. The seed had been planted, and my heart desired to know the truth. The word "private" hit home, and it made me feel low. I had never been addressed with such a negative tone before. I felt lower than a human being. This was the start of what would become a continuous sequence of events. The real United States Army was about to hit me like a jet plane. The question of whether I would be ready remained to be seen. It was told that I would be heading to the Calvary. The days ahead seemed even harder. The movie days of the Calvary were coming. All the strange things I had encountered before seemed to be nothing compared to what I was about to encounter. I was in a deep state of depression at this time, and the fact that I was a long way from home was beginning to set in. Now, to know that I was moving into the land of the horses made my life just a little more hectic. At this point in my military career I had not really found a mentor or a coach. I was out there on my own. In the midst of all that depression, the inner self was poised and ready to make my mark on this part of the Armed Forces.

I moved on down to the ultimate duty station, and now, like never before, I was in the United States Army. After some six months of adjustment, I finally had arrived at my first duty station, Schweinfurt, Germany. I called this unit the land of the Roughriders. I saw the horse and wondered if I would ride it. That remained to be seen. Upon my arrival, I found the United States Army's Roughriders hard at work. It became very clear to me that this was no ordinary unit and that the stories about the field were true. This unit lived in the field, and I did not welcome that with open arms. I had obtained the Personnel Administration Military Occupational Specialty just for this very reason, not to live in the field. And to find out that the next 24 months could be spent in the field sent my depression into a deeper state. I still was excited about performing my duties as an Administrative Specialist. I went to my first Personnel Administration Center and began what would turn out to be an arduous road of events within the administrative field. Taking care of soldiers is what my Non-Commissioned Officers drilled into my head during my inprocessing. It was made clear to be where you were supposed to be" would keep you out of trouble. I stayed in my room for the first few weeks after work and soaked in my loneliness and boredom. How sad it was to be such a long way from home with no one friendly to talk to. To say I had an attitude would be an understatement: my attitude was deep, and it showed during the first few weeks of my performance of duty. I was not attentive to what I was doing, and therefore I was moved from job to job. I felt I was being singled out at first, but I soon realized I was just acting childish. I needed to grow up and do it quickly. The day had come for me to put away childish ways and become the Man I was meant to be. One day a fellow subordinate gave me some important advice: **"You can stay in this room and have a miserable two years or you can get up and make the best of this tour."** Either way you are going to be here for the duration of the tour. It was at this point that I made a critical decision that jump-started my military career: I was here, and the time had come for me to make that mark I dreamed of and the fulfillment of the vision I received. I started making the best of my tour, and all the things around me began to change. I learned the value of a change of attitude and what a positive outlook could do for you even in the worst of situations. I began to learn my job well through a variety of job changes, and the knowledge I was obtaining was making me into a well-rounded administrator.

The pace of the unit was starting to pick up, and something started to happen that was not pleasant. I saw a number of Non-Commissioned Officers starting to get punitive action taken against them under Uniform Code of Military Justice (UCMJ). They started losing their rank, and this scared me. For the first time I saw, what I labeled as "the negative aspect of the United States Army." I had never dealt with any legal matters during my tenure of duty. Yet my curiosity was peaked because of the many reasons they were losing their hard-earned rank. I just thought once you had it, then you never lost it. Fear of losing my rank haunted me for the next few months. In light of this new revelation of the legal system, I made a commitment within myself to learn all aspects of the administrative job. I strongly felt that with the knowledge of how all aspects work, then I could prevent any part of that system from hurting me. There was also a strong yearning inside of me to aid other soldiers in their battles also. Here I stood with about 1 year in the United States Army, already thrust into the war- zone of administrative actions. I was Private First Class/E3 at this time and found myself in the job of handling Promotions. I had an invested interest in doing well in this job, for it could prove to be the key to me getting my promotion. The field duty was extremely cold, and sometimes I could not even feel my feet under me. I began to see my superiors falling short of the administrative requirements that were expected of them. For the first time, my eyes began to see some of the incompetence that my superiors exhibited. The fact that they had been in the United States Army for some 10 plus years was not being exhibited in the knowledge of their assigned duties. Therefore, in the end, it was the subordinates who suffered. To top the fact that we were not being taught was the fact that our ranks were being threatened. They constantly made us feel like we were the problem. I felt that this kind of action was not symbolic of leaders standing up for their own actions. My faith in the leadership started to phase fast over the next few weeks, and at one point there was a pact made with the E4 and below subordinates of the Administrative Center. We began to band together within each other and not allow our leaders to penetrate that band. We performed all our duties and stopped informing our leaders, because they had clearly demonstrated no interest in knowing. And all this was done because we were not being taught as we should and yet we were being blamed for the ignorance of our leaders.

The very leaders we had been taught to respect, were the very ones that could not teach us our jobs. I was astonished to find that my Non-Commissioned Officers were not efficient in their administrative duties. This alone led to many fearful moves for my fellow soldiers and I. To make matters worse, they would try to instill fear within us about it being our fault. I saw that if I were not careful, my superiors would make good on their threats to take my rank. I began to research the regulations and learn my job like never before. I felt within myself that there was a need to build up credibility outside of the superiors and I immediately worked toward that goal. I began to help more and more soldiers, and I spent more time at the higher headquarters asking the questions needed to tone up my administrative skills. The knowledge that I obtained over the next four months proved to be an invaluable asset to my survival when the Personnel Administrative Center came under vicious attacks. The superiors felt that the quality of service being rendered was not sufficient and not of the high caliber the soldiers deserved. My supervisors had managed to bring shame to the section by falsifying some documents in order to obtain benefits not authorized. At one point there were only subordinates running the entire Personnel Administrative Center. The quality of service was tremendous, and I felt it caused our new leadership to have a hard road to follow. They had already lost the confidence of the superiors because of their predecessors' actions. They were closely being monitored, and the knowledge they showed was always tested. To my amazement, the inability of my supervisors to provide the technical knowledge needed by the leadership, the more visible my abilities became known. This turned out to be a plus for me in the upcoming months. I was promoted to the rank of Specialist, 9 months in advance of the normal time frame. The Leadership found them coming to my fellow peers, and I to get what they needed, with total disregard for the incompetence at the supervisory level. The punitive actions continued, and I felt that many of them were unfair. The cases were full of misleading facts, and it seemed clear to me that a sense of fairness did not exist. *It seemed to me that you either had their ear or you had their sword. The one thing* that became clear to me was that there were different treatments being administered to Enlisted Corp versus that administered to the Officer Corp. This was mind boggling to me, and I began to take notice of a lot of things that I was blinded to in the past 15 months. The quality of service received by a small portion of the unit was top-notch compared to that given to the larger portion. It was clear that Officers received services that Enlisted Soldiers only dreamed of. I did not know the reason why, but I began to see more and more that there was something terribly wrong with the "one standard for all rule". I inquired through asking administrative questions in the legal field, the answers I got assured me that many soldiers had lost their rank due to ignorance of what their rights were.

To see a soldier lose his rank was just like having a bullet in the chest. These were not ranks in the grade of E4, and below being lost, but the grades of E5/E6. I knew that the time it took to obtain these ranks were 4 to 12 years. To have them taken away led to some devastating results in some of those soldiers' lives. Some had families and this reduction in grade proved to be fatal on their income for the family. This truly had an adverse affect on me in many ways. I saw a lot of the injustices occurring because of the very organization I was a part of: the Personnel Administrative Center.

CHAPTER IV

THROUGHOUT ALL THE TURMOIL

THROUGH ALL THE TURMOIL that was happening in the Rough Rider territory, I was steadily progressing up the grade chart. In an environment where soldiers were losing theirs, I just seemed to be going up the ladder of success. I was in awe of how my progress in the rank structure was coming so quickly. We had gone through several Non-Commissioned Officers within the Personnel Administrative Center, and that allowed me to excel in the daily duties of the Administrative Center. **Performance was at the forefront of the decision to send me before the E5 Promotion Board.** The thought of being a part of the Elite Leadership Core was very exciting to me at a young tender age of 19. I reached my birthday, and what better present to get than passing the Promotion Board. For the entire month of March, I dug deep and studied. I was determined not to let this opportunity pass me by. The massive amount of study material was overworking me at times, yet I was willing to persevere through it all to master another pillar in the dream and vision I had received from the Lord. Finally, after spending my birthday studying, the time was upon me to perform at the Promotion Board. I was somewhat scared, and that was evident when I first went into the Board. Sweat was dropping from my face, and that amazed me somewhat. Here I had worked with all these Board Members on a daily basis, and now you would think we were all strangers. They did what they had to do to calm me down. I went on to pass the Board, and had a great jubilation within.

I was on the verge of making my greatest accomplishment to date: Join the elite Leadership of the Enlisted Corp of the United States Army. After some three months that dream came true. **I was a young twenty-year-old Non-Commissioned Officer, and that turned out to be the highlight of the tour of duty with the roughriders**. For the next six months, I would endure one of the hardest transitions anyone could ever be asked to bear. Having to lead those who you have been a part of for the past 18 months, took tenacity. It was those inner challenges that brought out the Leadership within. It brought to life the glimpse of the road up ahead. I had a challenge that would test my inner abilities as a leader, and most of all as a man. I always wanted to be accepted as a Man with a character that rendered selfless service to my country. One of my greatest moments as a leader was while dealing with the United States' Flag. The rules were simple, and to the point: Never allow the United States' Flag to touch the ground. Having the responsibility of putting that awesome flag up and down was an honor. On this particular holiday, I put the flag up and then I saw it coming down. Without any help at first, I found myself having the crank for lifting the flag grinding my hand. I was determined to not let it fall. After what seemed to be an eternity, I was assisted in securing it. The adherence to what I had been taught just came to life when the problem arose. The life as a Non-Commissioned Officer had begun. I was proud to finally be a part of the Elite

Leadership Corp. It all seemed to happen so fast, yet I was in awe of what was happening. The positives were mounting in my young career, and that made me feel special. I knew where I was; yet the fact of where I was heading was still a big mystery. I was poised, and positioned to go on to the next adventure in my life. All around me was still a vast amount of turmoil. Being that I was a Non-Commissioned Officer I had no choice but to take ownership for what had occurred over the past two years. The feeling that it left me wasn't a pleasant one. I vowed that I would be the best Personnel Sergeant I could be. The foundation that had been set within me was a complex one. Soldiers reaching for answers from every direction. We had a new Command, and with that came a new philosophy of how to run the Command. Life in the roughrider's territory was changing, and it focused on more accountability for your actions. The shake up proved to be interesting for some, and dramatic for others. Being who I was, and what I had been through, allowed me to make the adjustments with ease. I was growing up amidst a whirlwind. The house was beginning to fade out, and the emphasis on training took on a new meaning. Being the expert was also at the top of the priorities. It was clear to all involved that times had changed. The emphasis on legal action dissipated also, and that caught my eye. For the first time, I experienced the power, and affect of a top authority change in a Command. The adjustments by all in the Command would make you believe the President was coming. Then, as I looked at it again, it was equivalent to the President in our eyes. You knew when he was in the area and the atmosphere had taken on a dramatic mood swings. Everyone wanted to shine with a good impression.

Against All Odds! I was focused on the mission ahead, yet I knew that meeting the challenge would not be an easy one. The commitment was there, and inner abilities were locked within this very heart of the young black soldier. I had a chance to look back over the past two and a half years, I saw a revelation I had not seen clearly during my tenure of duty: many superiors of the United States Army operated on the facts of who you were. The rank you had, and most of all the position you held. Many of the time right and wrong did not play a major role in the decisions that were made. I had come to the establishment hoping that I would be a part of equal opportunities for a What I found it to be was one that showed only the strong survived. I had to deci how I would deal with this reality at my new duty station. I had already received th grade of E5, and faced many adversities at the expense of my superior's selfish desire This alone made it a reality to me, of the possibility of losing it. Because of th selfishness within some superiors of the United States Army. I was a young man, wit a mission: to stake out my place in this monumental establishment. I knew that to make that mark I would have to be alert to all that was going on around me. **I had the foundation and now it was time to build the rest of the house to completion.** The first building ground would come by way of Fort Huachuca, AZ. Here goes the youn man on his way out west! What a ride I had with the roughriders. Sometime it got o of control, yet through a strong desire, calmness came over me. Fort Huachu Arizona, here comes a young man from the heart of the country.

CHAPTER V

COMING BACK TO THE UNITED STATES

HERE, I found myself coming back to the United States after a grueling tour overseas. It was a great relief to find myself back on American soil. I proceeded home to visit my family in whom I had not seen in two years. The good thing about being from overseas was that I felt closer to home, and the thought of not being there when an emergency arose was almost ceased. At this point I had an in depth taste of the United States Army and the way it played the game of life. I knew within I had to dissolve the knowledge fast I had obtained. And come up with strategies to combat many of the obstacles I would face at the upcoming duty station. Survival had been the key during my first full tour of duty and I felt proud of the growth I had achieved. I had played the game of life and survived where the roughriders abode. I had seen time and time again how the Chain of Command showed no regard for the regulatory guidelines. The pressure of this magnitude nearly had a negative affect on my attitude. I was forced to master my administration skills and make sure both the command and soldiers were aware of the truth. Accepting this task would not be an easy thing, but their was a deep inner desire to find a way. There had to be a medium where both the Command and the Soldiers benefited from my administrative abilities. I did not have all the answers, but the desire was there, and I knew the solution was on the way.

Despite the fact I had no implementing power, I knew I could have an affect on many of the decisions made. Being the "Expert" was my solution to dealing with all the upcoming adversities within my career in the United States Army. After spending some quality time with my family, I headed for my first Permanent Duty Station within the United States. The name of the post was Fort Huachuca, Arizona. I was assigned to a unit as the Personnel Staff Non-Commissioned Officer. I found myself working directly for the top Enlisted grade of E9 and what a challenge it would prove to be. I had grown to understand how the top of the chain of command worked; it was pretty much my way or no way. The directive came down and many of the subordinates dare questioned their commands. To make matters more complicated I found myself working for supervisors whom were civilians. The changes at this duty station were of a whole different caliber. Nothing in the present was the same and I was determined to perform. With the training I had received over the past two years, the question was, *could a unit of this unusual circumstance survive the training received by me in Rough* Rider land of Germany? It had been instilled into me as a soldier/Non-Commissioned Officer to do the right thing regardless of what others desired. Being that I was the only administrator within the unit, I had an opportunity to really make a difference in the administrative areas. During my last tour of duty I had at least three other Non-commissioned Officers who were my superiors, and they were go-betweens with the commands. Now I found myself having to work directly with the command. Something within me made me know that I was in the midst of a chaotic fire, the first supervisor from the command proved the fact " rank entitled you to have it your way."

He was deeply rooted into doing what he believed and some of those ideas greatly affected the soldiers in an adverse way. It was intense and controversial to say the least at times to absorb the weird philosophy of this superior. He was not tough, and another thing that made him tolerable was the fact that he did not compare to the superiors I had dealt with in Rough Riders Land. He was full of requests, but the forcefulness was lacking. With the moment of peace, I learned the systems, and tremendously broadened my administrative base of knowledge. I was allowed to do pretty much what my job required. Occasionally, I would execute training within the chain of command. During these quiet times, I made an asserted effort to get a broader knowledge base of all the basic facets of my job. That also included the legal aspects of my job specialty. I found some interesting facts about the legal system that confirmed that many soldiers were dealt a hand of injustice in my last unit. I regretted at this point, the fact that I had not taken this interest before. It could have alleviated some of those injustices from occurring. There were not many soldiers in the unit, therefore my ability to advise soldiers daily was limited. The trenches where I got my foundational teachings were in no way applicable to where I was now. In many instances, I thought I was not being as productive as I could be. Little did I know all this was about to change.

I had just come off some hard times outside the United States Army. The church had been an area that was not so kind to me during the past 10 months. The wounds and scars that I had received at the hand of the church had come full circle. I had endured many mind games that I could not see whether I was going or coming. Just the thought of the church could be full of mind games had never occurred to me. Needless to say I had taken about all I could take. With this upcoming change of supervisor, I knew that there had to be a change. I had received word about what my new supervisor expected when he was officially on board. I needed a little time to myself to regroup. Here I was a young man trying to find my identity and the very place you expect to aid you in that endeavor was full of mind games. I was near the breaking point, and it seemed like the incoming supervisor would send me over the edge. The one thing that was clear is that it was time for a change. I had endured many hard times, and they had taken their toll on me. I was in a withdrawn mode, a deep depressive state of mind, and the trickery tactics were coming from all angles. The church had taken my mind through a rigid set of ordeals that made me feel not worth living. It all had come down on me, and I had to get away. I took a trip home, and it was during this trip that I purchased a book that was the source of my rebound. It was a Bible, and that was the dose of medicine I needed to lead me out of the cloudy life I was living at that time. My state of mind started to un-cloud itself as I began to sort through all the incidents that had occurred during the past 10 months. I had decided to change something that would prove to aid me a lot in the upcoming months: Close my mouth and open my mind to seek out the truth. With my mouth closed, the trickery did not work anymore.

I knew that I was on the road back to living the dream and vision for my United States Army Career. To close out this stage in my life, I was a wounded and full of spiritual scar. The desire to end life as a whole was on my mind. Yet through all of the trickery and mind games my spiritual knowledge base had been further enriched with wisdom and understanding. The whole ordeal had given me the understanding that while the past 10 months had been laid back as far as the United States Army went I let my guard down. The letting down of my guard allowed the enemy to attack me from another angle: the church. The intent was still the same, to take me off course of the road leading to the vision and the dream that God presented me. The time had come now for my supervisors to start back cluttering my mind with their selfish desires. I thank God for the wake up call that got me back focused on the vision and the dream. The let down of my guard proved to be costly, yet I had a renewed focus of the vision and dream and the laws of my new supervisor had been laid down personally to me.

Near the end of the year of 1983, there was an anticipated change in my supervisor's position. The atmosphere totally changed, and I knew my ability to stand my ground as the expert was about to be tested. The message was clear from the start." What I say goes and that is the end of it." The flashback of Rough Rider Country came to my mind, and I could see it happening all over again. My understanding of why so many soldiers were wrongfully given legal action was by attitudes, like the one I was about to encounter head on. The party had only lasted about 10 months, and now the time had come to see how solid my foundation was. The ability to stand up and proclaim what was right was on the horizon. I knew the kitchen was about to heat up to a boiling point that would force me to react to a hostile environment. The word was out that my soon to be supervisor was already making his presence known throughout the unit. But it did not cause me to change my state of mind. I was poised and ready because I knew it was just a matter of time before we met head to head. It was not long before my supervisor started to make his presence known. He went to every department, and laid his laws down. I got my chance with him and within, heard every word he said. I was ready for whatever came my way. The method of approach was still the same: Do the right thing, and continue to be the absolute expert in the administrative field. My present state of mind did not make me want to deal with this immediately. The leader of the Enlisted Corp was about to lie on me as a young Noncommissioned Officer of 18 months. Life for me was hell and I did not have a desire to fight anyone at this time. Here we go, a new era with dramatic dilemmas.

CHAPTER VI

THE BATTLE: UNIFORM CODE OF MILITARY JUSTICE

NATURALLY, I did as I was supposed to do as a Personnel Administrative Non-Commissioned Officer: I advised him of what the regulatory guidelines stated and left it in his hand. While in his hands, he made the determination that I must have not understood the guidance that he had given out upon his arrival: Do as I say. The tension started from the start, and the egotistical attitude of my supervisor was in full affect. I would stand my ground and do my job no matter what. The relationship between the two of us was growing more distant as he pursued the struggle for total control. The next three months seemed like a lifetime for me as the Personnel Staff Non-Commissioned Officer. I found it hard to perform my daily duties because of the fact I spent most of my time in confrontations with him. Things got so out of control that an attempt was made to stunt my growth in obtaining the necessary requirements for my present grade. The stage was set for this battle to escalate to a personal level. The relationship between my supervisor and I had grown so bitter that he was determined to get at me one way or the other. I saw him as a threat to my vision and dream at this time. I would confront him head on. I was about to have my dream and vision tested. The plot was centered on me going to Primary Leadership Development Course. He was very adamant about the fact he did not want me going. I did not confront him directly, but through our struggles with each other I had grown to become stubborn in nature. I informed my superiors that he did not have a legal reason why I could not attend the course, and I would be going. The superiors agreed and passed this message on to him. He was furious when he heard this from my superior. The hostility grew deeper and I was determined to do my job no matter what. The stage was set and I was poised to go to the Primary Leadership Development Course (PLDC). Being that I had already been promoted to the rank of E5, there was still a need for me to go to the Primary Leadership Course (PLDC). My superiors notified my supervisor that I would be attending the next course, he informed them that he did not want me to go. There was nothing legally that could prevent me from going until he became very adamant that one way or the other he was not letting me go.

All of a sudden, I found myself in my superior's office being read an Article 15 that had been requested by my supervisor. After receiving this action from my superior, I was furious and somewhat in a state of shock. The Bureaucratic legal system was creeping its ugly head up again. Here I stood in the midst of what my superiors knew was a personal attack on me, yet none of them had the inner ability/guts to do the right thing. After some three and a half years of service in the United States Army, here I had my first personal encounter with the legal system. Personally, I felt that all involved knew that this was not right, yet none of them stopped the action from going forward. There were some charges that were clearly unproven within my eyes and I just knew I would prevail. Little did I know that I was about to be introduced to the legal maneuvering within the legal system. This was all new to me and I really did not know what to expect. After going to legal to get counseling, I felt uneasy after leaving the lawyer's office because he had only told me what punishments I could receive. This was proceeded by him asking me: "Do you want to choose a Court Martial?" Of course I said 'no' and that was the end of the legal counseling I received. The services that I had received from the Legal Office further enlightened me on why so many soldiers were wrongfully given legal actions. The expectation was that I would receive help in fighting my case, yet I only received information that I was already aware of. I knew what the superior giving me the legal action could do to me. To know that I would have to choose a Court Martial to get any more assistance was appalling in many ways. I did not know all the consequences of a court-martial, but I knew it would be a grave mistake to take this simple matter that route. I knew that I would not lose my rank and only 7 days pay could be taken. Beyond that the only thing left was a maximum of 14 days extra duty and restriction. I meditated and came to the conclusion I would have to fight this matter on my own. As I begin to try to get others to speak on my behalf from the unit, I saw the fear instilled within their eyes. Here my subordinates, peers and superiors had such a strong fear of his power and authority instilled within the unit he was in charge of, that they would not risk coming under his wrath as I did. The emotions within me were boiling, and I knew this was not right but what could I do? Along the way to the proceeding, I got a good piece of advice from one of my fellow soldiers: "You have to learn how to use the system, not try to beat it". These words seemed to calm me down and made me look at the situation again from an objective manner. During my evaluation, I compared the consequences of the requested legal action to the affect it would have on my dream and vision. After that in-depth analysis, I understood that the affect was really of non-affect. The struggle between Professionalism and Personalism was at war and a choice had been made to let Professionalism prevail in this matter. I decided to go in alone and present my case and let the chips fall where they may. I had an inner peace within that no matter what, I would be a better soldier because of this adversity. I was given 14 days extra duty, and lost 7 days pay for one month despite the fact that my superiors knew my supervisor was doing this to keep me from attending Primary Leadership Development Course. I was very disappointed in the way the proceedings had gone and I felt the urge to ensure that I learned the legal system more in-depth.

I was determined never to get in that helpless state again. The two hours of extra duty was performed down in my office. The words given to me by my fellow soldier to use the system and not try to beat it were rooted in my mind. The first day of extra duty brought that to life with my superiors. I was informed to go buff the floor along with a lot of other tasks. I politely informed my superiors that the Legal Regulation clearly stated that I was not to perform extra duty that degraded my grade. Having that knowledge within me enabled me to do my extra duty in my work place. The lesson learned was that if you do not take the time to find out what your rights are as a soldier, then you will always find yourself being abused. Through this ordeal, I had a renewed attitude of what being the absolute expert will do for you in the midst of adversity. After performing my extra duty, I thought within my mind it was all over. The greatest test for me during this time was how would I respond to the actions of my supervisor? I continued to advise him on the various administrative matters. The tension had settled down and that did not strike me as odd, at first. I requested to go on leave, and to my surprise, it was upon my return from leave, I learned that I was about to be reassigned. It was approved with no friction. The reason behind doing this requested action was very alarming to me. I had no clue why it was happening, but I did know it was not genuine. I took all the necessary precautions to ensure that I did not face another legal action upon my return. My attention to details had intensified and I was very cautious, while performing my duties in a professional manner. My supervisor had requested that my slot be changed to another Military Occupational Specialty.

This was one of the lowest moments in my career thus far. I felt that all the United States Army had taught me to do, was the cause of all the negatives that was happening now. I was taught to do the right thing, and now it was the right thing that was causing me to be moved. I loved what I was doing and to have that taken from me, because of someone's selfish desires was mind-boggling. The legal action did not top this last act of vengeance by my supervisor. I had just about completed Four years of Active Duty Service and it seemed as though the bottom was falling around me. Despite being hurt and upset, I did not make any effort to fight the decision. At this point, I was wounded with some scars that had not healed. At a young age of 22, I wondered what and why all this was happening to me. The desire to continue on was not gone, but at this very moment I needed some time for the wounds to heal. I had learned a valuable lesson during the past 18 months: Within the United States Army there were many that would not do the right thing. They were about power and domination over all they could achieve it with. They used the system that was established by the United States Army to carry out their personal vengeance. Overall, they just found that power was at their leisure to do as they pleased with no regard for who got hurt in the process. Do as I say or suffer the wrath of me. I received orders to go to the Signal Battalion and what did I know: This tour of duty was about to take my life through more twists and turns.

CHAPTER VII

TIME FOR CHANGE: REPORTING TO THE SIGNAL BATTALION

REPORTING TO SIGNAL BATTALION proved to be interesting. The fact that I was a Non-commissioned Officer gave me some say in where I was assigned in the battalion. After a few days of absorbing leaving the past crisis, I found myself in the midst of another one at my new unit. It was ironic that I had been in the United States Army for four years and had no award or recognition for any for my selfless service rendered. I did have the Legal action to show for all my hard work. I was all into my career as a United States Army soldier, and the level of experience was starting to make me a force to be reckoned with. I had endured many adversities and knew there were many more to come. The events that were about to transpire would change my life forever. I had already been under the monitoring of a few members within my church. They had heard me make the statement in 1983 that the Lord would send my wife in the upcoming year. That revelation had come through a general conversation. Little did I know that the love of my life was on the way to the Signal Battalion. The reassignment was all a part of a dream coming true. You see, in the previous units, I had no dealings with the outside units, so the reassignment was the key to the fulfillment of the vision. I had very little going on when it came to adversity within my military career at this unit of assignment. It was clear that I was about to be given a new challenge of exploring marriage. Here I was a young Man trying to make an exit from the single life at the tender age of 22. My military career had thus far been foundered. The road to the close of the vision was some 16 years away. Thus far I had attained the rank of Sergeant/E-5 and that accomplishment made me want to fulfill the vision. Time passed by and it seemed that the year was about four and a half months deep. Then at the end of the fifth month of the year there came a young lady that caught my eye. I saw the prophecy coming to pass. How this vision would come to pass I did not know. I had no clue how I would get from the meeting point to marriage proposal. Our first meeting was at the church I was attending. I offered her a lifesaver and was told hastily, "I don't want one." I then proceeded to my seat and left the situation alone for the moment. After a few more days had passed, people began to pay the relationship some attention, despite the fact the connection had not been made yet. The speculation of whether this was the wife I had been promised was clearly the topic of many conversations. The thoughts going through my head were mixed. *I felt within that she was the one, yet I had no clue how to get it all started.* It seemed that this little drama had taken the attention in the lives of a few people within the church. I was introduced several times to this young lady and it was like those who surrounded us, were setting up the union between the two of us.

News came down that I had to attend an orientation class for the new unit I had just arrived in. That within itself was where it all began to fall in place. The young lady was in the class and I was poised and ready to make my move. After the first day of the orientation, I offered her a ride back to the unit. Again she refused the second offer I had made. She chose to ride on the military vehicle and I made sure I got right behind the truck and followed it back to the Battalion area. It seemed as though I was making no progress with the woman of my life. I went to sleep that night, and then morning arrived. During the second session of the orientation, I started writing a letter to this young lady. It seemed as though I was possessed about getting the love of my life on course to the ultimate goal of marriage. The nature of the letter was rather bold. It declared to her that she would be my future wife. The rest of the letter seemed to be the icing on the cake. I gave her the letter and underlined how bold I had been in making it known the Revelation that my future wife was here. I proceeded to respond and I knew that I had taken a bold step, but I knew in my heart it was right. During the rest of that week, there were few words spoken between the two of us. I had many thoughts going through my head about that letter. I knew it had a positive affect, because the feeling on the inside said, things are about to get heated.

Over the next few weeks with the aid of my surroundings cast the young lady and I to begin to talk on a steady basis. The conversations were very general. I did not bring up the fact that she had not responded to the letter. After about another month, she had found her way to spending time with me in my barracks. We were also going out to lunch at her favorite place **"Peter Piper Pizza"**. The one thing I could always count on us eating was "Pepperoni Pizza". To be honest, I did not care for pizza, but I could live with it. I then proceeded to pursue the next step in the process: How to propose marriage to this quiet, young lady? She was not a lady of many words. I had known her for about four months. We then began to talk about the ultimate quest of marriage. It was clear that this was not your typical relationship. It seemed to be obvious that the two of us had the same goal in mind. All I knew was that the woman of my life had arrived at the scene and I was ready to make the move. I had no doubt that this was a moment, and only God could have brought such a wonderful couple together into a holy matrimony of **Love and Sharing.**

CHAPTER VIII

THE WEDDING IN THE MAKING

THE WEDDING IN THE MAKING: The subject of marriage was hot and heavy during the third month, which was August 1984. It seemed as though the fact of being engaged was not the topic of discussion. The days in the barracks had grown long as we watched her favorite shows. The days were long as we continually watched the TV shows; one in particular was the Jeffersons. I was literally watching my life forever changing before my eyes. The young lady had some hobbies that were not favorites of mine. One of them was bike riding. She loved to ride for long distances. Our conversation on this issue was very short because I had no intention of riding for that long of distance. The rest of our day ended for her with a "**Hot Fudge Sundae**" with nuts from McDonalds. It was very clear that Peter Piper Pizza and McDonalds would become a major part of our lives during the upcoming days. The road to marriage started picking up the pace during the month of September. We had for the first time come up with a date to make it a reality. The interesting thing about this date setting was that we had not purchased any rings yet. I had pursued this ordeal over the past four months and now it all seemed to be coming together. The tentative date was set for Valentines Day. What an awesome way to enter into marriage than on the Love Day of the year itself.

How awesome it would be to marry on Valentine's Day. The fact of the matter was that we were already making wedding dates with no rings in sight. This was about the fourth month of knowing each other; October was on the horizon. It seemed as though the community was beginning to realize that marriage was in sight as some things begin to take place. My wife to be found she was attending Tupperware parties and pretty much bought the whole book. It was a sign to me that I would soon find myself standing before the altar ready to say I do. Meanwhile, I was continually trying to work on the wedding rings. Money was not exactly plentiful during that time frame. Talk began to surface about a new car for my wife to be. I went on the scouting with her, and we finally agreed on getting her a Renault Alliance. Things were heating up during the month of October 1984. The date was drawing closer and it seemed to be so far away. We managed to get the marriage license and then it seemed for certain that wedding bells were about to ring.

The month of November would prove to be the month of it all coming together. I managed to get the rings and proposed engagement along with marriage at the same time. There was just one twist to the whole matter; the date all of a sudden changed to **January 12, 1985**. I was excited and ready to walk the isle. Things were all ready and set; it was just a matter of getting it all together. Bridesmaids/Brides men were being established. It was excitement all in the air as two **Young Black soldiers** were about to leave the single life. We both were somewhat scared and as the time grew closer the tension begin to boil from within. The pleasure of giving up your freedom you had enjoyed for over twenty years was about to be gone forevermore. It was time to get this show together and I had many reservations about the cost of this unique wedding. The outpour of love from within the church community was overwhelming. There were so many volunteers that were offering their help freely. We seemed to have accumulated a church decoration committee, in which we had to pay nothing. The atmosphere was electrified, as the two young people were tying the knot, after many speculations this would never come to pass.

The time of this event was fast approaching and I knew that my life would never be the same anymore. Furthermore, the life of my wife to be would forever be changed. She was about to become the wife of the controversial Young Black Man in the United States Army.

It seemed that all the military distractions had settled down for the moment. I felt as though God had smiled on the both of us to be able to make a connection that would change the way the world viewed marriage. Being the unique person that I was, I seemed to be handling some of the notifications of this marriage in strange ways. I wrote a letter to my parents and that was not the nicest way of letting them know about the marital plans. Others within my family just kind of stumbled into the information. I was set on having this day be one of the most memorable moments of my entire life. In my eyes, I was about to achieve one of the ultimate goals in life: marriage to a very beautiful Black Woman.

The certainty that this was the woman for me was never doubted. I even knew that amidst all the tensions that was brewing within the two of us as the date grew closer, was only a normal part of the pre-marital phase. Many of those around me were just as excited and anticipating seeing the event actually take place. There had been many speculations on which I would actually marry. To date, all of them turned out to be wrong, and to some there was a little bit of disappointment for the decision I had made.

December was upon us and things were really moving at a stressful, yet slow pace. The wedding date was set and it seemed that this event had finally been edged in stone and was a true go. The fact that a Young Black couple was about to wed to each other seemed to have a sentiment about it that was all in the air. **Here I was: a 22 year-old Black Man who was about to marry a 21 year-old Black woman and make a go of marriage in the United States Army.** How it would be was only a matter of days away. This was all new to the two of us and we anxiously awaited the reality to hit us both in the face. It was some six months later after we had met, that we were about to embark on the marriage of a lifetime for the two of us. I had no desire to wed anyone else, I was assured within my heart that this is what God had in store for me.

I had declared it over one year ago and the time had come for it to come true. Things were beginning to come around and the year of 1984 had come and gone. All that stood in the way of this marriage connection was 12 days. The program was set and all came to the conclusion this event was really about to take place. The supporting cast had played a vital role in bringing this event to pass. The key players were excited and anxious at the same time. No turning back was the word as we moved 6 days into the New Year. The final touches were applied to the program. My beautiful wife to be and I realized our single days were about to be gone. **The last days were long and there it was, the 12th day of January 1985.** That morning when I awaked knowing soon I'd be the husband of a beautiful young Black woman. No dreaming and I knew it was happening.

The time had come for it all to take place. I had not seen my wife to be for the last 24 hours, but I knew without a shadow of doubt that she would be walking up that isle within the next 3 hours. The practices had all been completed and now it was time for the real thing. Ten o'clock rolled around and here I was about to ride off to the church where it would all go down. I was still excited and knew that it was all about to come true. I had the Tuxedo on and now all that was left was to go to the church and await the walk of my beautiful bride down the isle. 11 o'clock had arrived and there I stood at the church where it all would go down. The supporting cast surrounded me and I could see the excitement within each of their eyes. They were all willing to help; yet none of them had any clue of what the two of us were about to get into. 11:30 a.m. came and it really started to get intense then. Everybody knew they had a part to play and was anxiously awaiting the entrance of the beautiful Bride, which were only minutes away. I was patiently standing at the side door awaiting my cue to come in and stand at the altar. The longest 15 minutes of my life had just passed and I got the word to come on out with the aid of my best man being beside me. The prelude was over and the time had come for me to see my beautiful Bride. The music started playing and there she came into the church at a very slow pace. I had my eyes focused on her every move and this was about to be one of the most beautiful days of my life. The walk was very slow and I enjoyed every minute of it. With my eyes attentively set on my future wife, I could just relish all the moments knowing that America was about to add another beautiful young Black couple to the ranks of the married. She finally arrived to the altar and the commencement of the **Holy Communion** began. The ceremony was a beautiful one and I was finally able to hear those words: "I now pronounce you Man and Wife." **The long awaited marriage of the beautiful young black couple was finally official. WOW!**

CHAPTER IX

EDUCATION FINALLY COMES: PRIMARY LEADERSHIP DEVELOPMENT COURSE

THE TIME HAD COME to finally attend the Primary Leadership Development Course (PLDC) in March of 1985. The teaching that I received at the PLDC would prove to further mature my military career forever. The in-depth teaching answered many questions that I had over the past four and a half years. It even brought back to my remembrance all the events that took place during my tour in Germany. I had seen many of the PLDC graduates encounter problems upon their return from the school. To hear the words of the Instructor as they taught each class, shed light on the reason why they had their problem. The words were: "We are not here to teach you how your unit operates, but to teach how thc United States Army says it should." These words alone let me know that I was about to learn many things about the United States Army. **"The way it is"** and **"the way it should be"** executed proved to be the foundation of the whole course. It was shocking at times, but for the most part, I was just receiving understanding of all the experiences I had over the past four and a half years. Being that I was E-5 made me the veteran of the class. Thanks to my supervisor in the year of 1983, I was not able to attend this course some eighteen months ago. Nevertheless, I was here now and that made it a dream come true in many ways. The Drill Instructor over my group was an E-5 and that would lead to some friction throughout the course. Here I was, getting an important part of the puzzle complete.

Finally, I was getting ready to add quality teaching to my foundational experiences of the past. The day by day teachings brought out many inner feelings. Some were pleasant; however, others made me go through all sorts of emotions. It was annoying to see how such a short course could stir up so many emotions inside of this soldier of four and a half years. It seemed as though for the first time, I was being introduced to how the organization I joined in July of 1980 was really all about. I learned so much about the organization named the United States Army that I felt like I was joining this organization all over again. The many questions I had over the years were being answered one after the other. All I knew was that when this course was over, the life as I knew it would be totally different in all aspects. I had a clear understanding of what the United States Army stood for. My anger turned into an intense desire to implement what I knew to be right. Germany was my next duty station and I was committed to handling matters different than in the past. I was accountable for the information I was receiving and that led to the inner conviction to make a difference. I knew and understood the mistakes others had made once they left the course. They tried to implement the real United States Army openly. That only caused them to fall into the wrath of their leaders. I vowed from within to implement moment by moment. **With all the controversy I had received during the last four and a half years, I was fully prepared to take on my second tour in Germany. I had vowed**

to not let this second time around be like the first one.
During the PLDC training, I had many off-course conversations with Leaders who gave me some valuable information about the cunning ways used within the United States Army. It was during this time of conversations that started my eyes to look at the structure of the United States Army. **Hearing these old Leaders share some of their struggles gave me a taste of how difficult the road ahead would be for me as a "man" others would see only as a "black man". I began to see the racial profile of the United States Army like never before. It was clear to me that blacks did not enjoy some of the prestigious positions that Caucasians held. To further enlighten me, I got the understanding that the few positions we held were not out of voluntary change, but forced change in America. It hit me that these Black Soldiers/Leaders had endured over the years many acts of racism in the way of social decisions.** Sometimes, **racism is not done by individuals, but by decisions** that are made and adhered to. The **Racial Profile** of the **United States Army** made it clear that when the **decisions** are made, most of them are **racist** by the very fact of who makes up the **Racial Profile** that are making them. **The Racial Profile of the United States Army could and does lead to racist decisions being made.** This fact does not conclude that all making the decisions are racist, for that is far from the truth. Sometimes, discrimination is accomplished by who you do not have there during the decision making process. A clear example of this is when you are making a decision about how female soldiers should be dealt with in certain situations and do not have experts of those situations, the final decision will be bias. The very fact that there was no qualified representation led to this set of decisions. Therefore, the same thing applies along the Racial Lines; the Racial Profile of the Leadership in the United States Army does not allow **equal representation** for all races involved.

How enlightening this was to me as a man, human being and most of all as a soldier in the United States Army. How sad it was to know that blacks served in the United States Army and didn't share equal status with our white counterpart. Also they could not hold valuable leadership positions because of their status. Abilities did not play a major role in decisions in this racial era of time. I took the time to absorb all this *information and still press on within myself to make my mark on the United States* Army as a Man. I realized that I was only one, but behind that one could make a difference for all. I had no way of verifying this information received, but just looking at the leadership structure over my past four and a half years of service made the information credible. (Added experience to all that was said, and here it was that the first leader since then had been of my race.) Shocking upon looking back on it. There had been various Black leaders in the Enlisted Corp, but they had very little input in the decision-making process As a Personnel Noncommissioned Office Administrative Specialist, I saw first hand who made the decisions. Unfortunately, there was little representation from any other race than the Caucasian race. The facts were clear to me that down in the trenches there was no **balance of power**. Therefore one would *have to conclude that this would lead to injustices along racial lines. I learned a lot of* information from the black Enlisted Leaders at the Primary Leadership Development Course. **I felt my whole frame of mind was being reversed through all the information I received over a 30-day period**. The phrase **"Leader from the back of the line"** came to mind. I knew at that moment that I had found the way to balance the two tasks of taking care of the Chain of Command, as well as, the soldiers at the same time. The philosophy: "Take care of the soldier, you take care of the Chain of Command." came alive. I soon graduated from the life-altering course and prepared to leave again for the foreign land of Germany. **How awesome the past thirty days had proven to be in my United States Army career.**

CHAPTER X

ON THE ROAD AGAIN: FOREIGN LAND OF GERMANY

THE DAY had finally arrived for me to depart to the foreign land of Germany. The news had already been revealed that our Joint Domicile assignment had been messed up, and another dilemma was that my wife was pregnant, and my presence was needed. I had not a clue where I would be stationed, but regardless of where I was, I had plans to reside with my family from Day One. I was anxious about getting this new adventure on the ready-to-go-line. As I boarded the plane to head overseas, I had over eight hours to entertain deep thoughts. The questions of how I would get my Joint Domicile in an active status was on my mind. How was I going to get this done was totally unknown at this time. I was focused on handling all the changes that had occurred with me, and I had to adjust to the changes quickly. Here it was some 2 ½ years later that I was on my way back to the land of Germany. My spouse had been on the land for some three months, and it was time for me to regroup with her. This time I knew what it all about and was focused as I got on the plane. I already knew that when I arrived at the unit there would be a confrontation. The Administrative Department had messed up our joint- assignment. This had caused us to be stationed over 50 miles away from each other. The only mission at hand was getting to Germany and reuniting with my spouse. I did not know how the unit would deter me from accomplishing this mission.

After arriving toward the foreign land of Germany for the second time, I was processed and sent to my duty station. It was clear from the first meeting with my immediate supervisor, that this tour was going to be a long one indeed. I quickly cut to the chase and informed him that I had to get to the train station to unite with my wife in Hanau, Germany. The boldness that I talked to him with, seemingly startled him, and yes came out before he knew what he had said. It was at that point that I was looking racism and discrimination in the face. My inner being said this tour of duty would truly be an educational one. It brought back to mind the prophecy I had received during a Prison Ministry Service that our church rendered. Upon learning that this was my last time at the service, they desired to pray with me. Many in my church thought it to be strange that a group, who we were being ministered to, would return the favor. Especially being in jail, what could they have to offer? At this point, the prayer prophecy began to come forth: "They expanded on the fact that during this tour of duty I would be abused by my superiors, but through it all, God would exalt me in the end. I was encouraged to keep the faith through it all." In that moment, when I saw the looks in my supervisor's eyes, the word "abused" came to mind. I knew the prophecy was from God and now I had to find a way to endure this upcoming abuse. This started my new era in the land of Germany. Again, the look in his eyes was negative. We did not have many words, and soon I was on my way to the train station. The road to Germany, for the second time, would be a long one.

The speculations were starting to surface in the air about the battles I would face during this tour of duty. I had established the fact that I would be staying with my spouse some 50 miles away. This decision would cause me not to be able to participate in the Physical Fitness Training on a daily basis. I was exempt from it from the start and this did not sit well with my supervisor and others within the command. With my spouse being pregnant, there was not really much they could do about it. I would catch the train back and forth on a daily basis. From the start I knew that this was not going to work out over a three-year period. I noticed that many within the command were giving me strange looks. I was not very sociable at this time because I had my family situation on my mind. The baby was due in a few months and I had to get a resolution to this delusion I was facing daily. The arrangement to miss physical training was not a popular choice, to say the least. I had gotten things in order, and the veil was lifted. Being that my family was about to be with me, I was primed and ready for the battle like never before. Within the administrative office, there were many deceptive things happening. At the company level, things had really heated up with all the complaints. I just thanked God for his intervention in getting my family together and prepared to do my tour of duty. All things were about to commence.

The expectation was just what the word was Expectation. The original assignments for my wife and I were totally messed up. We found ourselves many miles away from each other. For the first month, I would take the train to my duty station. This went on for about a month then my car arrived, and I drove the 50-mile drive daily. It was an interesting dilemma that I found myself in. Here it was that my wife and I were miles apart and that this was not going to work for a three-year tour. I began to make some noise about how our original assignments had gotten so messed up. My superior officer was young, and when he got word of the information, he went with it. He made some phone calls to the highest authorities. Within a few days, I got word that my wife would be coming close to where I was stationed. The matter had been escalated so high, that it was solved faster than normal. I was excited about the fact that she would be coming, and she was ecstatic that it would all be happening. The only thing we had to do was to get the paperwork through the proper channels and make it official. This seemed to be somewhat hard, but it did materialize over a period of about a month. The system had again come through for my family and I. Despite all the negatives going on around me, this act gave me a calm attitude. It was the priority of having my family together that consumed my time. With the paperwork finally complete, I was ready to whole heartily deal with all that was happening within the unit. Things were beginning to heat up at my unit. Soldiers started to complain about the fact that I was allowed to come to work late and I did not participate in physical training because of the long drive.

CHAPTER XI

A 'BOUT' WITH RACISM

WORD came down that I could no longer miss physical training. There were very few words that were spoken between my supervisor and I. He clearly understood that I was not the type of soldier that you could push around. That was the understanding factor with him choosing me not to be the Personnel Staff Non-Commissioned Officer (PSNCO). It was clear to me that my supervisor did not see me as a man with knowledge, but he saw a man who had no right to stand beside him as the Personnel Staff Non-Commissioned Officer. All qualifications were clearly met by me for placement in the position. I had been in the grade of E-5 for three years and now found myself working under soldiers who had been in the United States Army for three years. Here I stood, in this organization, as the senior Non-Commissioned Officer under my supervisor and really had the skills to perform the job. With all that knowledge, my supervisor made a bold move: allowed a totally inexperienced Non-Commissioned Officer to enter the position. The affect of this move could have proved to be devastating for me, but the remembrance of the prophecy received allowed me to endure this matter professionally.

The professionalism did not take away the inner feelings; I was upset and felt that this was a deliberate Racist Act. It seemed that all the views on this matter were coming to the light through the actions of my supervisor. There was also a feeling of depression that was embedded within me: I could not help but think that it could be me that caused his action. After some reflection on that thought, again I came to the conclusion that he did not see me as a soldier with qualification to perform the job, rather he saw me as a **"Black man"**. This was the barrier that he could not get over. It was personal and did not reflect the guidelines of the United States Army. I was in the midst of closing the deal on my family coming together. This issue was very sensitive to me, but I chose to leave it alone for the moment. I was excited about my family soon coming to join me. The fact that I was soon to be a father made it all the more exciting. At times, it was those two thoughts that enabled me to endure the day to day adversities on the job. To add to the scheme of my supervisor, was the fact that he had the command supporting him. The reasoning that I had attained over the past five years was about to be challenged against a powerful opponent. I had faced many adversities over the past five years, but never had I faced adversity of this magnitude. I felt like I had been placed in prison and told not to speak. Without the position, I was helpless when it came down to enforcing the standards. I saw many things that were being done wrong and I could not do anything about them. This would prove to be the most depressing fact that would haunt me through this whole ordeal. Day after day, I heard the command carrying out actions against soldiers that were against regulatory guidelines. I could not but feel guilt within over the shortfalls of the Personnel Administration Center. The knowledge and wisdom that I had within made

me feel accountable.
Soon, my family joined me at my duty station. The timing was perfect for me, and I was very fortunate thus far in my military career. It seemed that every time a scheme seemed to close in on me, there was a way of escape. After three months, we were finally together as a family. It was time for me to get into doing my job. The tension between my supervisor and I had escalated over the past few months. Over the past three months, he had silently acted as if I did not exist. The communication was non-existent, and the affect of that was about to come full circle. **I had laid up many nights meditating over what I labeled as "degrading acts of racism and discrimination". Knowing that the entire command knew of his actions made me realize that this racism and discrimination was blatant. I could not believe that a command within the United States Army would condone such an action, yet it stared me in the face. I was the recipient of the racism and discrimination and the feeling deep within was not pleasant.** The abuse prophecy was in full force. I was wrestling with many issues daily. I was an outcast with no home and that equaled to a lonely feeling of degradation. In attempts to further humiliate me, I found myself being confronted with various weigh-ins. For the first time, my weight had become an issue. The stakes at this level were beginning to increase to a higher level. Little did I know they were about to start an epidemic within my military life. I was unfazed that I needed to weigh in. Up until this point, I had never really evaluated my problem with weight control. There was not much emphasis placed on that subject during the past five years. Now it seemed as though a light came on and said, begin the weight control program for life. Here I was found to be overweight, and the negative turn of the Command started to rear its ugly head. The reality of the matter was that I had become an enemy of the Command. They knew that I spoke what I felt, and that was not the kind of Sergeant they wanted. I was placed on some jobs that I would do on my own. I was not under the Supervision of the Personnel Staff Non-Commissioned Officer because I outranked him. I was just excited about my baby on the way.

Finally, the day had arrived, and it was time for my first child to be born. The date was **November 14, 1985**; it was a day. Here we go again, another addition to the family. I knew our lives would never be the same. The adjustment to having a child was new to us both. Both of us had to adapt to new sleeping habits. Being in the military was not an easy task since the child came along. All the work that came with the birth of the child caused us to totally reorganize all our schedules. Appointments and other various tasks required me to miss work hours from the job. The adjustment was being forced upon me quickly. I was in the midst of learning to balance my responsibilities to the United States Army and my family. The word dedication comes to mind as I searched for that median. No matter how hard I tried, each time family matters had to be attended to, resistance was received from my supervisor. To add to the negatives being accused by my supervisor of neglecting the United States Army allowed the intensity within to emerge constantly.

CHAPTER XII

THE UNIT'S MISSIONS HEATS UP - MOVING HIGHER

THE UNIT'S MISSIONS were heating up, and it was time for Field Duty. A greater degree of emphasis was being place on the Field Training phase of the unit. Being that both my spouse and I were in the Military, there was an issue about both of us performing field duty at the same time. An agreement was made that we would never go at the same time. That released a lot of pressure from both our frames of mind. Meanwhile other things were happening. I would soon get my first introduction to what would grow to be a "thorn in my flesh", the Weight Control Program. Finally they had succeeded in finding me to be overweight. Now I found myself in the Weight Control Program for the first time. That fact alone made the revelation hit home like never before: you have increased responsibilities and more than you will be affected. The presence was now at an all time high because of the high stakes involved. The life I had enjoyed for the past five years was over, and I needed to make some quick adjustments in how I dealt with certain matters. All adversities that I faced now had an affect on the others who had become a part of my family, meant I had increased responsibilities. I realized that the decision from here on out affects others you care for. Reality was starting to set in many ways. The fact that I was now being entered into a Weight Control Program made it become more real to me. Here I was with a wife and a kid, and being told that I could be chaptered out of the United States Army. My supervisor had all things under control as he went about doing his daily tasks. The degrading system was in full effect and I knew that my days up ahead would not be easy.

I saw many things being done that were contrary to the regulating guidelines. Control was my supervisor's desire and he knew it would not prevail with me in charge. At this point in my career I was conditioned to just take care of my area. Supervisory skills had not been utilized that much over the past 5 years. Most of my time as an E-5 had been spent without soldiers under me. I felt within myself that I had met my **first racist** in the **United States Army**. It was his actions that made this racism come alive. Yet it was the response of the command that made me know that racism and discrimination was alive and well within the United States Army. The task at hand for me was how do I respond to his bold acts of racism. I made the choice to do my job to the best of my ability. Through all the adversity that I had faced over the past 6 months, my performance of duty was top-notched. I had always controlled any areas of responsibilities that I was in charge of. Being the absolute expert was the matter that was embedded in my daily walk of life in the military. The areas that had been assigned to me were accomplished in an outstanding manner. The Evaluation Reports was my primary area of responsibility. I developed a quality tracking system and maintained it daily. I did not allow my superiors to have access to my system, yet I made sure all reports were processed in a timely manner. The only way to obtain a commendable rating on Command Inspections was with zero reports being late. I was well on my way and was determined not to allow one report to be late. All my other assigned duties had very little impact on the day to day operations of the Personnel Administration Center. I was still in such a degraded status in the Personnel Administration Center that I felt helpless as soldier after soldier came in for service. No matter how hard I tried to ignore the vicious acts, they would constantly weigh my mind down. It was there in my mind where the battle was always energized. I just continued to keep myself busy so the acts of racism and discrimination would not get me down in my daily outward acts.

The command had just went through a rigid Command Inspection and I had managed to get a "commendable rating" in the area of Evaluation Reports. This achievement further mandated that my abilities were warranted in the PSNCO position. This accomplishment pretty much forces the hand of the command when it came down to appearing before the E6 Promotion Board. Being that I had just come off the high during the Command Inspection, my supervisor had no choice but to recommend me for my attendance to the Board. That **racism and discrimination** was so active in his heart that he was determined to never have me work under him as the Personnel Staff Non-Commissioned Officer. It was during this sequence of events that it all came to the light and was clearly seen by the new superiors in the command. He had a plan and implemented it. He recommended the Personnel Staff Non-Commissioned Officer for promotion also. I studied and prepared myself for the upcoming Board of **April 1986**. For the second time, I found myself preparing for a Promotion Board during my birth month. In an attempt to maintain the stronghold on me, my supervisor also sent the current PSNCO to the same Promotion Board.

SOME 4 YEARS LATER, I attended the E-6 Board and excitement was in the air. We both passed the Promotion Board and thus, allowing my supervisor to keep him in the Personnel Staff Non-Commissioned Officer position. The day that I passed the Promotion Board was the conclusion of another piece of the puzzle. E-6 was next to the last rank that I had been promised within my vision. Meanwhile, there was a second child on the way, and that made the new rank very important. The second child was on the way about five months apart from the first one being born. I had come from a big family and it seemed that we were heading in the same direction. The road out of the abused status was coming faster than ever. Frustration started to really set in with my supervisor. I did not know what it was all about, but things were clearly not going his way. For the first time, he was losing the power he had enjoyed previously to the new Command's arrival. I started listening and found out that his time would soon be no more.

The future of the PAC was in a chaotic state and relief was needed. To my surprise, the prepared replacement for the PAC was a soldier already in the command. Another part of the puzzle started to come together. The soldier taking over the PAC should have been there already. There had been a clear conspiracy by the old superior that moved him into another job. Total control was their desire and they were determined to get it at all cost. In the end, the change was made, and there was a transition period. It was during that transition that a heated conversation came up about the Personnel Staff Non-Commissioned Officer position. The outgoing supervisor was trying to persuade the incoming supervisor to leave things the way they were: he clearly stated to him so all could hear: I am going to make him Personnel Staff Non-Commissioned Officer because that is the way it is supposed to be. Finally, there came justice after dealing with the racism and discrimination for some 16 months. He had already been within the battalion. The first thing that he took care of upon his arrival to the Personal Administration Center was to make me the PNSCO. The standards that had been set by me had shocked the entire Command. The abnormal results were clearly out of character with how my superiors had portrayed me to the command. My contact with the command was very limited because of the fact I was not in a leadership position. The dedication to duty had started paying off for me as a soldier. I had beaten the weight control dilemma and my performance of duty was outstanding within the limited responsibility I had. Many times, I had wanted to just go off and there was something within that did not allow that to happen. **Here it was that I had been in the Command for some 16 months and now things were happening faster than I could comprehend. Just when I thought it would never end, here I stood officially as the Personnel Staff Non-Commissioned Officer of the command.** Out of all the negatives I had faced in my military career thus far in the command, I had constantly continued to perform at a high level. The hard work paid off. The wonderful thing about this whole situation was that I had grown to have a great working relationship with the supervisors in the other five companies. The relationships that I had developed with them made me at ease about working with them in many ways with my new derived position. Things could not have been any better at this moment. I was rightfully in my proper position and the command was about to experience a different caliber of soldier.

Yet, in the midst of all that, I was glad that my new supervisor had the inner ability to do what was right. He knew from first hand knowledge how my old supervisor had degraded me. He had watched me endure the struggle of working for someone who had less time in grade and definitely less knowledge. Despite the wishes of the outgoing supervisor, he chose to do the right thing. These move alone made an impact on the whole battalion in which I was serving. What had been would be no more. This move had a positive affect on my self-esteem at that time. I knew my inner abilities, yet I always seemed to find myself questioning myself on whether all this was my fault. To see this act go on for an arduous period of time had started to have an adverse affect on me as a soldier. Knowing that your abilities were being abused made it all the more unbearable. Yet, at this point it all seemed to be coming together. I knew that the upcoming months would be my time to shine as the Personnel Staff Non-Commissioned Officer. The sad thing about the whole ordeal was that the struggle over the past 16 months had caused me to have some doubts about my inner abilities. Through all that doubt, I was now poised and ready to take this challenge on head to head. In the midst of all this, the date for my second child was quickly approaching. So much was going on in the young life of the 24 year-old soldier. **For the first time in my life, I had found myself in the middle of a battle with my inner self. I was still left with the question of why my old supervisor had done this horrible act over this 16-month period. As I looked back on all the actions during this time period some things began to come clear. I realized that my inner abilities had no affect on the decision. It all boiled down to the reality of how he could not separate the one fact that hindered him from doing the right thing: he saw me as a "Black Man" and his racist belief could not allow me to be placed where I rightfully belonged.**

The conclusion to the whole matter was that during the rest of my military career, I had to deal with many whom would not accept me to be a "man", but see me as a "Black Man". This revelation was a hard pill to swallow, but on the other hand it brought this chapter of my life to closure. How sad it was to know that the inner abilities were overwhelmed by color of a person's skin. I had choices to make and I knew that whichever way I chose to go would have consequences. This racist act by one individual has caused me to choose whether I wanted to be known as a **man,** or just a **Black Man**. I did not take long to decide my choice: I was going to be a man that just happens to be a Black Man. I was determined to strive for perfection as a man in the United States Army. I wanted to be known by the contents of my mind. The consequences of this choice, I knew would prove to be dramatic, full of negatives, and most of all "Controversial!" The joy of being finally second in charge was deeply appreciated. The time had come and I had the weight under control and things seemed to be going well for me in that department. With the events of the past, I was not going to allow anything or anyone hinder me from making the most of this opportunity as Personnel Staff Non-Commissioned Officer. All the injustices I had felt helpless during the past 16 months were history. Now was the time for me to make a difference in the lives of many soldiers. The Administrative Department of this Command needed a quick overhaul. The care of soldiers was lacking and that was about to change.

Meanwhile the month of January 1987 came around and the entry of my second child was on the way. The baby was finally born on **January 20, 1987**. Here, I had two boys and life at home was about to get more interesting. The challenge of both being in the service was about to be even more complicated. There was a new job, bigger family and now a command of soldiers lacking help administratively. I wasted no time instituting a system that aided soldiers in taking care of their families.

CHAPTER XIII

SEEING MY LIFE CHANGING - SECOND IN CHARGE (POWER)

I COULD SEE my life in the United States Army changing day-by-day. The adverse affect of the degraded treatment I endured was creating a genuine concern within to ensure soldiers did not go through it. I was committed to the welfare of soldiers and the command did not like that at all. I felt like I was there to speak for them, when they could not speak for themselves. The Command was really becoming uncomfortable with my style of leadership. I was also constantly working toward obtaining my promotion to E6. I had completed many correspondence courses. The month of May was approaching and I was about to put in a reevaluation promotion packet. Then, to the surprise of all in the Command, in **July 1, 1987**, cut-off scores came out. I was selected for promotion to E6 through them. I had worked 7 years to attain this prestigious rank. Little did I know that the road would be full of twist and turns. Some of my superiors did not like the fact that I was where I was, so they began to put the pressure on me to perform. All the expectations got harder and that within itself made me work harder. I had no doubt that it all started from the fact that their injustices toward me had failed to hinder my growth in rank. It was becoming clear to them that this man who happened to be a "Black Man" would not be denied.

I started mastering the knowledge for my job with great determination. I knew that it would not be very long before I would have to explain every decision I made. Correspondence was a part of my life and the time had come for me to validate my promotion packet. My superiors were so set on proving how much I was doing wrong they were not prepared for the shock wave that was about to be thrust upon them. The word came down that I had met the cutoff score to the grade of E6/Staff Sergeant. I was excited and it did not sit well with some supervisors in the battalion. Word had spread quickly that I was about to be promoted to the grade of Staff Sergeant. The whole Chain of Command was in shock, because I made little noise about being in a promotable status. As usual I accepted the promotion graciously and thanked the good Lord deep within me for the promotion. I knew to date it was one of my greatest achievements. As I looked back on the first seven years, I had to take deep thought about the struggle I had endured thus far. To say I was looking forward to the next 13 years would be a grave understatement. I had more questions than answers deep down inside. I felt this was about to be the most complex transition within my career. The adversities thus far seemed to have placed me in the position where I had to learn how to walk within the hierarchy of the United States Army. The stakes were higher now and my durability was about to be tested. All the rules were changing before my eyes and I just knew there would be many rough days ahead. The road to twenty years was going to be an uphill struggle. The family was growing at this time and a third child was on the way. The size of the family was growing and the intensity within me was burning as the prophecy was coming to pass.

burning as the prophecy was coming to pass.

New superiors began to come into the battalion and this was not good news for many in the command. The changes the battalion was going through caused a tremendous change. The new superiors were checking out many things. I had gone ahead adapting to the new superiors with a low profile approach. I went to great lengths to make sure my enlistment in the United States Army was reached without any stumbling blocks.

The opening came for me to reenlist for a six-year time span; I jumped at the opportunity. It was accomplished on a leap year date, **February 29, 1988**. I was secured within the United States Army for another six years. I was totally hyped about completing a dream that I dreamed of: Being a retiree of the United States Army. The time was approaching for me to leave Germany, and things were changing all around me. I was glad that my new ETS date would take through 14 years. And to top that off, if everything went well I would only have to reenlist one more time to meet my retirement date. The time grew near for our return to the United States. The incoming assignment was somewhat confusing. I had reenlisted for Fort Sill, OK and it seemed as though the United States Army wanted me in Ft. Bragg, NC. A tour in Germany was about to come to an end. Here, I stood as the man who had endured so many struggles during the past three years, and still was seeing life in a positive way. It was almost too good to be true. I then started to take notice on a few reports I was doing on a monthly basis. Despite the fact that I had done them for the past nine months, I had never looked at the report with the attentiveness I did now. Through the in-depth look, I noticed something that put me in a state shock at first: I was in the midst of a struggle that had the odds against me from the start. For the first time in my career I looked at race record in the United States Army. The numbers on the statistical report on race enlightened me on my struggles over the past eight years.

Here it was, eight years in my career, I found myself under a leadership class of soldiers who were predominately Caucasian. Then, as I looked back at the struggle, it made me even more startled and alarmed. The clarity of the reason of the struggle began to sink deep in my mind. I was trying to be and do something that was not done by many black men in the United States Army. It was as if I crossed the bounds while doing my job. I then realized the playing field was not a level one. My attitude changed dramatically after my realization of the revelation. During my present assignment, I got to observe three leaders of the Black race. One of them was ultimately kicked out of the United States Army. The other one was rendered helpless by the Chain of Command. The last one was the only one that yielded positive results because the position he held was a position acceptable for his race. To top all of that, I now had power and authority. All of this labeled me as a "Black Man" trying to make a difference as a Leader. I had changed. Deep down inside I knew my upcoming years would be full of adversity. I had signed seven Evaluation Reports and never gave much thought to the Support of the **Equal Opportunity Program**. I asked

myself, what do these words really mean within a military environment. I had more questions, and was at this point in my career I wanted to pay closer attention to the racial profile within the United States Army.
There, at the end, I began to realize the massive amount of attacks I had received as a Staff Sergeant. I started to become very bold as a Non-commissioned Officer. This was a side of me that many of my superiors had ever experienced before. For the first time in my life, you can say I started feeling my authority as a Non-Commissioned Officer. The power and responsibility of being the Personnel Staff Non-Commissioned Officer (PNSCO) was coming full circle as I knew it. The boldness, in which I started to speak with, even surprised me at times. I knew that the awesome amount of responsibility I had inherited with becoming a Staff Sergeant would be extensive, controversial, and overall, a force to be dealt with by all.

THE POWER of being second in charge of the Personnel Administration Center was beginning to sink in. The responses of my superiors were also letting me know that something within me had changed. I was making more decisions and my input was bolder. Now that the revelation of the Racial Profile of the United States Army was visible to me, I began to see things clearer. With that, I also began to give clearer responses to the various adverse administrative matters. These responses clearly upset my superiors because it usually went against their desires. I was clearly defining myself as an individual soldier who spoke what he believed to be right. Many times I stood alone in my opinion of the matter at hand. I was further enlightened by many of my superiors who chose to keep their inner feelings on the matter to themselves. They just supported whatever the desires of the higher superiors were with no regard for what was right or wrong. This alone really puzzled me at first and made me upset with the supervisors within the command as a whole. Many injustices were done before their eyes and my superiors allowed them as a whole to happen without the fight. The position that I was in, allowed me to go to my top supervisors and voice my concerns on a one on one basis and the results were even more disturbing.

The sum of the whole matter was that we are here to support our leaders and not complicate matters with an opinion. This had a profound affect on my military career and I vowed to not let that mentality be a part of my way of doing my daily administrative duties. Then something else stood out and hit me like a ton of bricks. I was the only black soldier in the midst of all the supervisors. It seemed like I was a troublemaker and at times I doubted whether or not I was doing the right thing. I did more deep soul searching and clearly knew that it was not I, but a system in place that did not support right or wrong, only the desires of the superiors. The confirming factor that led to this conclusion was all the times I had experienced this very fact at my last duty station. The words came back to me that: I am here now and you will do what I tell you to do. I could not do that then some 5 years ago, so I definitely would not do it now. The fact that I could make a difference was becoming more evident day by day. There was a new phrase added to the equation of making a difference:

Consequence over the past 8 years, I realized that I had not been fighting for matters that dealt directly with me. Aside from the Article 15 in 1983, I really had an uneventful bout with adverse actions. So I was suffering for fighting the cause of other soldier who sometimes I did not even know. I had become a soldier's man and that was in line with the leader's duties and responsibilities. **Taking care of soldiers was my business and a lot of people did not like it at all. So the mode had been set for my upcoming days: being a soldier's man would lead you to many long and complex days. Knowing that only made me desire to take care of soldiers even more. Here I was with the ability to make differences in many families' lives *and I would not let it pass me by.***

UNFINISHED BUSINESS ON THE HORIZON I had no idea what Fort Bragg NC was going to be all about. It was near time for me to leave Germany and there was one piece of business outside the United States Army that needed to be taken care of. It was noted in 1984 that I accepted my calling into the preaching ministry and received my ministry license in 1985 as I departed from Fort Huachuca, Arizona. The outgoing Chaplain had made the decision that I would be going before the Ordination Board. This decision did not go along with the teachings of many in the Church. The noise that was being made was sickening coming from the mouths of Christians. I had endured a hard time at this church during the past three years. I was belittled in many ways, but I remained devoted to the church. All that devotion paid off at that moment when the Chaplain made that decision for me to be ordained. It caught me completely off guard and made all the hard times worth it at the same time. So amidst all the opposition from within the church, I was set on taking advantage of the opportunity that came through the channel of a United States Army Chaplain. I was excited and continuously studied and waited for the event to take place. The opposition of this event happening was the very one that had the task of ensuring that I got to the church where the board would convene. He was totally against the idea because of tradition within his denomination. They did not believe in ordaining ministers without the church calling them to Pastor. Nothing that came my way seemed to come through normal channels. Most of the positive things I had achieved during the past 8 years had come through adversities and struggles. Every promotion attained to date was in the midst of a struggle. All knowledge attained about my job was received from adversities that I saw many soldiers endure without any knowledge that they were being mistreated. Here I stood, again, head to head another struggle within the church. I often wondered why I was chosen to go down the path, but it was the vision and dream that kept me holding on despite of all the adversities and struggle? The vision was being fulfilled before my eyes, and a lot of new things had occurred in the past few years. This was a big move in my life and there were many times when I had to pinch myself to see if it was true. I was scheduled to leave Germany on the **6th of July 1988** and the board had been scheduled for July 5th 1988. There was no room for error. I was patiently awaiting my transportation and eventually we left. Nothing seemed to be going right. He acted as if he did not know where the church was. I just sat there knowing that this was in the hands of **Higher Authority.** Suddenly we made a right turn, and there was the church. The meeting had started and I was soon called in before the Ordaining Board. Through all the chaos that had proceeded me to getting to this point, it did not take my attention off the mission at hand. I was focused and ready to go in and do what I had been called to be a Man of God. It seemed as though there was no doubt that I would prevail at this ordination board. The one thing that was being tested more and more was my faith in God. All that I had attained thus *far made me dig deep within my faith and look beyond the adversities. The* **Ordination Board** asked me many questions and through intensive knowledge of the Bible, I was able to answer them. They gave me some situational questions and I answered them with what I would do. The vivid question that stood out in the midst of them all was when I was asked, "What I would do if I had to go counsel a female? Would you take my wife or not?" My answer was yes and no, I explained to them that it really depended on the situation. I would take my wife if I felt she could be of help to me in solving the problem. I further went on to say that I did not believe that as a Pastor I had to have my wife or any other female accompany me to see another female. The ordination board sent me out to deliberate, and after a while they called me back in to announce that I had been unanimously approved for ordination. Here it *was that under unusual circumstances, I had obtained one of the most precious* approvals that a minister could receive: to be an **Ordained Minister.** I was told that my paper work would follow me to the United States. I had seen that accomplishment come to pass. Who would have thought that a Chaplain in the United States Army would have recommended me for ordination? I just saw at work my awesome God and yet I wondered what would I have to endure with all these accomplishments in the future. The ride back to my duty station was a calm one and I found myself completing the last night of my tour in the foreign land of Germany.

July 6th, 1988 came and I went to the office to sign out, and as I reported to the office, my highest Non-Commissioned Officer Superior locked his eyes on me. We *did not see eye to eye on many things during our tour together. I looked at* him without saying a word, for our eyes said it all. He clearly displayed his feeling of hatred toward me as a person and a soldier. His eyes also conveyed that behind all that hatred, there was respect there for the inner abilities I had exhibited during this tour of duty. I also wanted him to know that there are a few soldiers who will stand up for what they believe, even if it meant standing alone. He did not say parting words and I did not either. Our memories of each other were the locking of eyes for the final time. Whatever negatives he had tried to bring my way were all diminished as I walked out of the door. I had managed to get out of a hostile environment and marveled at the fact there was nothing he could do. I was about to leave Germany knowing I had accomplished many tasks during the past three years. This tour of duty had set me in greater positions in both the Church and the United States Army. I knew that with all that responsibility would come some pain, suffering, scars, wounds and memories that

would forever set me aside from most who walked beside me during my career in the United States Army.

Thus ended my tour of duty in the republic of Germany via Mainz, Germany.

Fort Bragg, North Carolina, here I come!!!

CHAPTER XIV

FORT BRAGG, North Carolina (START OF A DYNASTY)

THE START OF A DYNASTY: As I prepared myself to make the move to Fort Bragg, NC, I had to come up with a strategy to avoid all the injustices I had experienced over the past eight years. The one thing that was for sure was that I would not be soft spoken when clear injustices were being carried out. The boldness that I had demonstrated over the past twelve months had netted me some positive results. Many of the soldiers had not received some of the negative actions that did not meet the regulatory guidelines. The other side to that was, I had created visible enemies from within the superiors in the command. The choice was clear to me: do your job and expect many conflicts with the superiors or allow the injustices occurring in the Command to continue and take on a selfish attitude. The trenches had been full of chaos and something within me just revealed that, to me this tour would be no different. I enjoyed my leave and we proceeded on to Fort Bragg, NC on July 18, 1988. Things started happening as soon as we arrived and the drama immediately commenced. The third child was almost due and the unit that I was assigned to was within a Training Command, which was of an elite status. The last place I ever expected to find myself was in the midst of a training establishment. To further complicate matters, I was in the midst of two Personnel Administrative Centers that were trying to co-exist at the same time. The idea of co-existing was not something that made me happy in the heart, and that alone was disheartening.

I knew within what I had to do: get those two Personnel Administration Centers functioning as self-sustaining entities. That would be easier said than done. I found my first days within this unit in a state of disbelief. The daily operation was full of chaos and left my mind in a state of frustration and full of anxieties. I had many issues with the lack of control of the students who were being served by the Personnel Administration Center. I was in an awkward situation and frustration was expanding day by day. I saw what I wanted to do and I knew it would not be long before I made it come to pass. **August 7, 1988**, the baby had come and now there were three children in the household. Things were heating up all around me and I knew some *changes had to come soon. The pressure was on and I knew that there was a war that I* had been thrust in the middle of. I could not run, move, nor did I understand why it was a war everywhere I went. I wondered if this was a war that would go on for the duration of my United States Military Career. I had to come up with a plan of attack, if I was going to survive this warfare.

Little did I know what I was about to encounter during the next 4 years in my life. The assignment was one that was totally new to me. I was informed that I would be handling the students of the Special Forces Training Center. The amount of students was about 10,000 students per year. The inception of the Student Personnel Administration Center was the beginning of a dynasty that would change the way students were taken care of forever. The service that is rendered within that Student Personnel Administration Center would be unmatched by any other personnel servicing organization. The diversity of operations within this organization would not be easily understood, unless you had hands on experience. This is how I viewed the separation of these two entities would grow to be. It all sounded good to me and implementation of this dream seemed to be impossible. I had to be so clever in bringing this dream to pass. During the first few months, I just observed the entire operation. There were many concerns that I had and instead of voicing them, I established solutions to implement when the time was right. The lost of training hours were mounting up, and this caused major problems on the turnover rate of the students. The fact that students were staying longer than expected, made it a high visibility area of concern for the superiors in the command. I saw my opening about to come and I was set to take advantage of it. After about four months deep into my tenure of duty, I took advantage of a moment in time, and made the announcement that would start the dynasty of a lifetime. At first it fell on deaf ears, but I would not let it go. The more the command kept searching for answers for the students' dilemma, the more enticing the idea begin to look. I was not so elated about their actions, because I knew they were trying to get the monkeys off their back. Despite knowing that fact, I wanted the dream to get into motion.

Finally toward the end of the year of 1988, the decision was made that the two Personnel Administration Center would become separate entities. I was totally ecstatic over this decision. The dream had finally come to pass and now it was time for the implementation of the plan. This is where things really got complicated for the entire Command. It was easy for them to commit because they had no answers on how to implement. As the first Personnel Sergeant for the newly formed Student Personnel Administration Center in the year of 1989, I saw a vision that would lead to the quality service received for years to come by the students of this Training Group. The problem further complicated itself as I started to make this organization a viable entity. I did not share much of the ideas that I had with those who were not focused. I had learned my lesson over the past 8 years about sharing your plans to the unreliable. I was devoted to implementing the greatest organization ever established. I wanted to take this organization from scratch to an entity that would be there for an eternity. The success that would be enjoyed came through the years would come through many arduous hours of fine tuning a diverse organization to service a wide-based diverse group of students.

The diversity of students within the school was immensely high. It was something that I had never experienced before. At first I was the Non-Commissioned Officer in charge with one soldier and one civilian worker. This type of system went against everything that I had been trained. It was thought that the success of such an organization was impossible. The massive amount of students was the focus of the opposition of the idea of two Personnel Administrative Centers not working. I knew from the beginning that the task I had chosen to undertake would not be easy. There would be a necessity for many arduous hours to start an organization from scratch. I saw this as an opportunity to make my mark like never before. Just knowing the affect of starting this organization from scratch made me more than determined to under take the daunting task. I had no doubt about my inner abilities to run a Personnel Administration Center of this magnitude. I was determined to let nothing stop me from succeeding at this goal. Here was the opportunity to make my mark in the United States Army. The start of a dynasty is what I saw this organization to be. It was my baby and I felt the time of delivery was at hand. All the odds were against me, yet I had been dealt that hand my entire military career. I wanted it and the determination to bring the Dynasty to life was about to get in motion.

With the aid of one soldier and four civilians, I begin to set in motion the Student Personnel Administration Center. In the eyes of many in the command welcomed the good intentions, but never really gave it half a chance to survive. And this brought alive the greatest establishment to ever be assembled: "***THE STUDENT PERSONNEL ADMINISTRATION CENTER.***" To say the truth: I was a happy soldier and one proud man in the United States Army. All that I had been denied to do was wrapped up in the creation of this unique organization. I knew the time had come to begin the arduous task of organizing this newly founded organization that would exhibit the quality resources and the service students deserved. I knew I was the right man for the job. I had the inner belief that once established, the next phase would fall in place over time. I had a dream in my head and was about to bring it all together. I proceeded with the assigned personnel and started devising an awesome plan to ensure that this organization would grow into an invaluable asset to the Special Forces Training Center. There were many issues that I had to confront head on during the inception of this new organization. I needed more personnel and that was not in the plans of my superiors. It seemed at times that the support received was not being received due to the anticipation that I would soon fail. I also tried to make another move that I would have a hard time getting support for moving the Student Personnel Administration Center from under the Permanent Party Personnel Administration Center's supervision. What I was asking for was a total disconnection from the Personnel Administration Center already in existence. I had managed to get the Personnel Administration Center separated; yet we still occupied the same building. I wanted this organization all to myself with no illusions or perception that we still abide as a **coheren**t entity. The word failures were leaking all around the Special Forces Community. I was forever shaking up the old way of doing things, with the new ideas for my organization. The obstacles were certainly mounting up against the administration center. I took on each obstacle one by one. It seemed that each time I eliminated an obstacle, the Chain of Command got angrier at my success. I would not be denied in my quest for the completion of my dream. The tenacity that I constantly demonstrated made it clear to the command that I could not be denied. I had a vision of the Student Personnel Administration Center being an entity within itself. As I eliminated all the negatives, the higher command superiors started looking at my idea in a positive manner. This did not sit well with my superior who approved the idea from the start. This made the organization realize that I was very sincere about the success of this new entity being started. They started to devise little schemes to attack my credibility and that proved to be a distraction from the task. I was determined to stay on course orchestrating one of the most unique organizations into a living entity. That caused them to awaken my thorn in the flesh: The Weight Control Program. I was so internally involved in the task at hand that I chose not to expend much energy on the entry in their Weight Control Program. I just follow their procedure and that was within their scheme, as they wanted it to be. I just wanted to see things within the established Student Personnel Administration Center get into an active state. Quality service being rendered to students was the matter I kept sounding out with to the higher echelon of superior.

Finally, I had the blueprint and it all was in place. The time for full activation was upon the feet of the command. The service that had been rendered to the training students thus far had yielded many positive results. I wanted to move my Student Personnel Administration Center away to its own building. The command saw my sincerity and granted my request. This act gave me the assurance that the Student Personnel Administration center was finally here for the long haul. All the critics were still angry and demonstrated that anger in many ways. I was heavily dedicated to the task at hand and did not allow much to distract me. The seed was beginning to grow and that made me feel good. I had grown in staff to having four civilians and two soldiers. I was still not content with these changes and I made another request. The request also called for a change in the rank structure of the organization. The present structure had one E-7 within the organization. In charge of two E-6s: I requested that each Personnel Administration Center have their own E-7 position. I was informed that there was no way that I would ever get this organization to buy off on that request. It was told to me that the request that I was continuously making was causing a great deal of stress at the higher level of the organization. The fact that the world as they knew it was changing before their eyes made them very uncomfortable.

I must take a moment to expound on the key element that troubled them. Here it was that a young and energetic soldier was talking an unknown language to the superiors. I was determined that the things I desired would happen; I was the expert, despite the fact that I was treading unknown waters, I had the confidence that it could be achieved; I had a dream, aided by a vision of the end product. These two things coupled together gave me the assurance that the impossible was happening. The next few months were filled with questions and answers.

CHAPTER XV

THE INNER DESIRE TO DO SOMETHING GREAT -NEW ERA DAWNING FAST

THE INNER DESIRE within me is burning because a golden opportunity has just arisen within the organization. We are moving from the current building that we work in. The meaning of this for me: was getting your own Student Personnel Administration Center away from the other Personnel Administration Center. That task was accomplished and now I could accomplish the awesome task I was about to encounter. I know that the superiors were waiting for me to complain, so I had to be a smart administrator. I started to establish guidelines and suddenly it became clear that this adventure was going to produce many headaches. The first employee that I was able to get as a part of the new Personnel Administration Center was the glimpse of hope that I was going to build on. There I was in my own building with most of what I had been seeking to this point.

Over the next few days after the holidays, I began to convince my superiors of the fact that I needed an organization of my own. The puzzle was beginning to come together. I found myself with a staff of the vision coming true. Immediately, I began in February of 1989 to begin to put together one of the most awesome organization ever started within the Special Forces Training Center. Being an expert within the administrative field, I took each issue/concern and secured them. The situations were coming fast and the prior preparation was starting to pay off. The inception of the Student Personnel Administration Center was alive and well, and the superiors started seeing that something was about to happen. The only problem was that they had no knowledge of what it was going to be. The type of administrative services rendered to the students was as different as day and night within the training group. The most arduous task was to try to explain the massive variety of soldiers' status along with the different requirements to solve each of their problems. So you can see here I stand with a dream and a vision of turning a monster into a smooth viable system. The Student Administration Center was the monster and it seemed that I had been chosen to tame it. The confidence that I displayed outwardly to my superiors was beyond reproach. Yet the inward doubts and questions was like a fiery furnace. I knew that if the dream was to stay alive, I had to move quickly to calming down the fire.

A massive amount of positive things started happening during the next two months. I had my first Personnel Staff Non-Commissioned Officer. This addition to the team gave me the missing military part of the puzzle. The leadership positions were E5 and E-6. That was the start of the vision of having the positions upgraded to E-6 and E-7. Despite the fact that I had my own Personnel Administration Center and building, I was still being rated by the supervision of the Permanent Party Personnel Administration Center.

During the month of May 1989, I was informed that I would be going to Fort Benjamin. Harrison, Indiana to attend the Basic Non-Commissioned Officers Course (BNCOC). This was to take place in July. I realized immediately that the first test of the stability of the Student Personnel Administration Center would be tested during the six weeks I would be absent. I had two months to purify the team that I had just gotten together over the past four months.

I started to concentrate on systems and instilled within my civilian force the confidence that they could perform those systems. I was a leader that believed in being in control: yet willing to allow my workers the freedom to be themselves. I knew that this would lead to a great controversy among my superiors. It had been voiced on many occasions that I had a group of outspoken employees. I would always ensure my superiors that there was no need to worry. The freedom to speak among themselves was healthy. My concept was as long as they were communicating, the build up of frustrations would be released. Here we are now with a group of outspoken civilians and a supervisor that believed it was healthy. The bonding within the Student Personnel Administration Center was beginning to become evident to the superiors of the Special Forces Training Center. The quality of service being rendered to the students was beginning to be noticed. The training time being lost was starting to decrease. This was a key element being tracked by the chain of command. I knew now that the key to winning over the chain of command was to continue to come up with more positive systems that would keep soldiers in training. There was no turning back at this point. Yet, I began to encounter another problem. The immediate superiors began to see a good thing happening and wanted to have their names in the spotlight.

The one thing that I strongly believed in was to keep my superiors informed on a need to know basis. I had learned through the years that knowledge in the hand of the wrong people could be dangerous. The key to my survival this far in this command had been their need to have me answer the unknown questions to their superiors. I instilled within my subordinates during the two months that they were the experts. I ensured them that they would be just fine during my absence. Yet, I knew they would be tested beyond measures they could ever understand. The dream was growing and many of my superiors were looking for the key ingredient. The last few weeks before my departure was intense, yet it was the most rewarding time as I look back on it today. I proceeded on to school. The chaos started before I even landed at my destination. The events during the six weeks have never really been told to its fullness. There was a massive amount of tension between the civilian employees. The outspokenness reached an all-time high during my absence. The pressure of the absence had an adverse effect on my Personnel Staff Non-Commissioned Officer. It got so stressful; that an act occurred that I strongly felt was out of character. The superiors were in full force to see if the new organization was stable. They found themselves constantly meeting walls that said back off. It was very annoying to them to constantly hear the words: this is the way my supervisor instructed/ trained us to perform this task. The events as a whole made my superiors realize within their minds that I had a strong hold on the Student Personnel Administration Center that could not be penetrated, despite the fact I was absent. This fact alone changed the whole relationship between my superiors and I.

Upon my return, that point was made clear through the famous words: "You need to get over there and take care of your Indians." You know there was a famous reply: "The Indians are not the problem because I'm here." Looking back, I can strongly say that is when the war began to become personal. I was recognized as the "Honor Graduate" during the graduation of my class, yet I was crowned as the dictator of the Student Personnel Administration Center upon my return. I, as Honor Graduate of the Leadership Course, made my immediate supervisors upset. I had proved again that I was the absolute expert in my field of expertise. I knew now more than ever that I was about to enter a war zone with my supervisor and superiors. The positives were growing on my behalf, and that did not sit well with the opposing forces. I had been energized and now more than ever I was about to take the Student Personnel Administration Center to higher heights. I had endured all the critics who deemed that this would never come to pass. I had clearly defied the odds and I knew that meant war with my opposing forces. Through all of the obstacles that I had overcome, the opposing forces had to accept the truth: The test had been massive and continuous, and they realized that these results were evident: We have allowed one of our Enlisted Soldiers to create an entity that only he held the key to its success. I had accomplished a feat that not many enlisted soldiers could do: START UP an organization from its conception to its life form. They all knew I had hit a home run, with me on the base. Therefore only I could and had the power and authority to run around each base. All the answers were deep within my inner being.

The system was established and instituted by me. For years to come history would constantly say This Student Personnel Administration Center stand as an awesome entity through the dream and vision of a man. My mark had been made and I knew and felt that this was a monumental accomplishment. The foundation had been set and I knew that all the other decisions would fall in place. History was in the making, and it all started with the idea of man. One of the greatest organizations had be totally shook up and would never be the same.

A NEW ERA was about to begin. During the early stages of foundering the Student Personnel Administration Center it became obvious that there was another shortfall that needed to be addressed to complete the Personnel Administration Center. The quality of service had dramatically impaired training time throughout for the students at the training group level. Now the time had come to focus on their loved ones. The students were still losing the valuable training as they traveled all over the installation to get their Military Personnel Record Jacket's taken care of. The answer to the question of how to solve this problem was to have a detachment from the Personnel

Service Battalion come down to the Special Forces Training Group. The one thing that I had to do was sell the idea to all parties interested. To the delight of all involved it seemed like the perfect solution. The issue was addressed and it was agreed that the Personnel Service Battalion would give the Training Group a small portion of their Civilian employees to run the Student Records. As the Personnel Sergeant, I had experienced many frustrations trying to get the students the unique service they needed and trying to balance out the many lost training hours lost due to appointments. I strongly supported having a Student Records, for it only catered to the needs of the students and alleviated immeasurably the amount of training time lost. The alliance that was formed between the Student Personnel Administration Center and Student Records was one that has never been experienced in magnitude, or that I have ever been a part of. Despite all the bugs/glitches that needed to be worked, I felt a sense of jubilation that something great was about to happen. The ideas of having these separate entities were met with some resistance, largely because of the transition work involved.

The forces that wanted to be in control were determined to break down the creator. Let the war games begin. I knew the coming days would not be easy, yet I strongly felt that the foundation was laid. With that in mind, I braced myself for the upcoming events. The atmosphere had totally changed and the opposition was starting to play hardball. The things that did not seem to matter became important matters. My leadership chain soon gathered, time of 1989 to mid 1991 was truly scheming against me as a team. There were many little things that were happening that let me know I had to be on my guard. The fact that I had demonstrated my absolute expert abilities in the administrative arena made them come with the attacks from other angles. They started to attack my supervising abilities through the subordinates and leaders that worked directly for me. Attempts were always being made to break up the solid team that I had developed. To their surprise, they found out that they did not care much for each other, yet they had a great deal of respect and loyalty toward me as their leader and supervisor. They soon realized that this was not the way to go in disorienting my abilities as a leader. Therefore they had to move on to another method of attack. One was to add the very thing they did not want to have during the establishment of the Student Personal Administrative Center, an E-7. Through my tenacity as a leader and man to stand up for what I believed, led them to feel a new leader would calm me down. So that added another notch to the greatest organization I had been associated with thus far in the United States Army Career. What was intended as a negative turned in to a positive very quickly. The other means of attack was through the weight control program. Here I had some 10 years in service and the thorn in my flesh had seemed to rear its ugly head again. I still stayed focused on the mission at hand, which would prove to frustrate them even more. At this point, I was no longer in charge of the Student Personnel Administration Center, for I had been downgraded to Second in Charge. The one thing that did not change was that all the knowledge of the Student Personnel Administration Center was contained inside my head. Despite the fact they did not care much for me, they did need me for the success as a whole They were constantly looking for the balance to hold me down, yet having access to the knowledge.

What a tricky web of circumstances, I found myself in the midst of. I was needed as an administrator/leader, but despised as an individual because I refused to play the game ascending to the established rules. I knew in my heart that when they saw the opportunity to make their move, they would. I just had the faith that no matter what their approach would be, in the end, I would prevail. Meanwhile, the Student Personnel Administration Center and Student Records was on a course providing some top-notch service to the students of the Training. There was a move made to take the supervisory authority away from me. I was informed that I would no longer rate the civilian employees that had worked for me. I strongly protested this decision and I did not use disrespect to get my opinion across. I informed my superiors that if they were not going to allow me to rate, then I would no longer be in a position to give them directions. This caught them off guard. The supervisory chain does not go down, it flows up. This fact made them withdraw that tactic to get control. The movement started moving toward what I labeled as personal attacks on me as a Non-Commissioned Officer. They began to pile up little things that were minor and attempted to make them major flaws in my duty performance.

It seemed to have been destined that this family would consist of six. There it was that the fourth child was on the way. I was well on my way to further adjusting to the new unit. Life at home was well adjusted with the three current kids. After some nine months the time had arrived. **January 17, 1990** and the second girl was added to the young black couple that wedded four years ago. The message was clear and contentment came to us both this would be the eternal size of our family. To have two boys and two girls was a gift from God. Now all that was left was to train and raise them to be able to survive when time for them to embark on the world.

CHAPTER XVI

THE ATTACK ON JULY 25,1990 - I WAS HOT-HEADED

ON JULY 25,1990, I was given a counseling that gave me a 30-day notice. Relief would be the end result if my duty performance did not improve dramatically. My response: "I, Staff Sergeant (E6) Ronnie Isom, am making the following statement concerning the counseling given to me on or about 1600 hours on July 25, 1990. First of all, an Initial Counseling was done, but the second quarter counseling for April 1990-June 1990 were never accomplished. The context of the counseling given on July 25, 1990 is derived from a lot of speculation, not facts. It is noted that there have been complaints about the efficiency of my office. In this environment, it is very difficult to evaluate complaints with the variety of situations that the students present on a daily basis. The complaint referred to in this counseling was investigated by me and found to be invalid. Academic Records has led this command to believe that its mission is so important that they cannot leave their place of work to ensure that they have what they need to do their job.

The Student Personnel Administration Center has become the scapegoat for Academic Records when their jobs are not done as they should be. No follow-up is done to show the validity of allegations made by my Peer Supervisor. Apparently as evidenced now and in past situations, if she says something it is assumed to be true. The complexity of the Special Forces Qualification Course leads many soldiers to have complaints arise from frustration. This command has a tendency to drive from perceptions, rather than gathering facts about situations that arise. As far as emphasis, my utmost emphasis has been to ensure that soldiers are taken care of, given the right guidance from the Student Personnel Administration Center. The chain of command makes it very difficult to enforce most of the directives from the school itself, in that it has never supplied concrete guidelines to the Student Personnel Administration Center. It is very difficult to enforce policies that are unclear. The reference to poor movement of paperwork to proper places is another allegation that no one has bothered to verify. The present system is burdening the Student Personnel Administration Center and Academic Records. They were a part of the in processing team until it was determined that their job was too important for them to leave their office for 30-60 minutes to get data to perform the job that had been assigned them.

Nevertheless, the Student Personnel Administration Center is constantly hearing that we are the cause of common knowledge that, as a Non-Commissioned Officer, I strive each and every day to anticipate and alleviate problems before they arise. Tracking and identifying potential problems requires communication through the whole administrative support channel. The Student Personnel Administration Center seems to be the center focal point for everybody within JFK SWC to blame his or her shortcomings on. Pro-active is a word that serves to be the slogan for the A Company,

Support Battalion, but it only applies to certain sections. It seems to be all right for some sections to be proactive, while others seem to get consoled when they fail to do likewise. Most of the disruptions encountered are not because of lack of planning, but are because a link in the chain is not supporting the Student Personnel Administration Center. Many things are always being done to reiterate that Student Personnel Administration Center is not important. Many allegations have been made that the Student Personnel Administration Center is totally out of control, yet not one in the chain has made any effort to come over to Student Personnel Administration Center and actually see first hand what the Personnel Administration Center goes through on a daily basis. I feel that very little support has been given to help the Student Personnel Administration Center to function within this environment that we have been chosen to work in.

The function of being responsive to the needs of the command is one that has been done for the entire time that I've been here. Soldiers are the driving force behind me being in the United States Army, and with or without the support of the command, I, as a Non-Commissioned Officer, have dedicated my career to ensuring that soldiers are taken care of administratively to the best of my ability. Now to address the problem of informing higher personnel, whenever problems have been brought to the attention of my superiors, the response has mostly been, "You don't understand the function of the Student Personnel Administration Center". When information is requested from me pertaining to administrative matters, my responses are always questioned. I am treated as if I don't know what I am talking about. I feel that the knowledge I've gained through ten years in the United States Army is not being used in the Personnel Administration Center, as it should be due to the fact that several times it is contrary to what the command is trying to be and do. They say do it by the regulations, and when I tell them what the regulation says, they always blow it off until they hear it from someone else. In order for this operation to flow like it should, the chain has got to let the personnel that the United States Army has trained, do the job they have been trained to do. My past/present performance proves without a doubt that I'm one of the top-notch Non-Commissioned Officers in the Personnel Field.

To summarize the area of emphasis Number 1, with the support of the higher immediate chain, the Student Personnel Administration Center could concentrate more on taking care of soldiers than always trying to prove whether or not complaints from other sections are valid. The responsibility needs to be put where it belongs, and that would alleviate a lot of the disruptions encountered by the Student Personnel Administration Center. Proactiveness needs to go across the board. An attitude is one area that has to be looked at from a new perspective. The chain has been constantly advised of the fact that I, as a Non-Commissioned Officer, am not being allowed to fully do what I have been trained to do. The ultimate result has been frustration on my part. I've tried to work with the chain and the NCO Support Channel, and I just keep hitting stone walls. Yet, I still take pride in ensuring that the soldiers are taken care of, but again no one has taken the time to actually see what the real problem is. The physical training here is one area that needs a lot of work when you talk about being professional and accurate according to regulatory guidelines. As for my interactions with my subordinates, there is no problem. Speculations/perceptions might say there is one, but statements from the subordinates would alleviate that allegation. I know without a doubt that I have been and still am a role model for the soldiers in A Company.

With my superiors, I have never encountered a problem from battalion level on up. The ones encountered with my superiors in A Company have been generated from the chain believing that I was just unaware of what the Student Personnel Administration Center's mission is. Through incidents that have occurred, it had become evident that some people in my immediate chain did not want to hear what I had to say. It seemed they felt I was challenging authority. My job as the Personnel Staff Non-Commissioned Officer is to advise them on the regulatory guidelines on actions they are trying to implement. That is all I have been doing, advising. I have been, and am still striving, to ensure that my military bearing is at a top-notch level. I have made great progress in the past two months and will continue to do so. I feel that the Weight Control Program needs to be looked at very closely to ensure that it is being run the way it should be. At the present time I don't feel we have a positive program. I am well aquatinted with how it is supposed to work, and I feel it only right to bring it to the attention of the command. I am physically fit and know that passing the Physical Readiness test will not be a problem. My overall appearance is amongst the highest in A Company, Support Battalion and will get to be the best in the very near future after overcoming some small obstacles.

In conclusion of my response to the overall counseling, as a Non-Commissioned Officer, I believe in soldiering, taking care of soldiers, in being the best Non-Commissioned Officer that the United States Army has. But, most of all, I believe in standing up for what I believe in no matter who does not see eye to eye with where I stand. I know the personnel Administration field inside and out, and I can and will be an effective tool in the Student Personnel Administration Center. I just need the support of the chain and the NCO Support Channel to help make the Student Personnel Administration Center the best operation in the Special Forces Training Group.

Let us put the "P" back in personnel and take care of the soldiers."

I WAS HOTHEADED at this time and I made many mistakes in giving out damaging information that was harmful to me. I was so administrative minded and headstrong, that I went into my superiors' office and constantly threw procedure at them harmful to me. The tension was at a high level and the professionalism was turning into a hostile environment. The civilian employees were constantly telling me to calm down and I being stubborn, stuck to my guns. I had encountered problems with my weight and this seemed to be the avenue that the superiors thought they would use to control me. I never let down and that made my superiors very upset. Unknown to me, a plan was on course and it would eventually blow my mind. I received two evaluation reports and they contained two false statements about my status in the Weight Control Program. I did not see the ultimate act that was being orchestrated. The Student Personnel Administration Center and Student Records was in full force and with about 2 years of operation as a separate entity. And things were beginning to come together and all of a sudden there was another attempt to separate the Man from the organization he had grown to love. It was time for the sad conflict to get started in the year of 1991. Word had come down that there was a requirement for an individual with my grade and Military Occupational Specialty (MOS) needed for temporary duty at Casualty Branch in Washington. It seemed like the perfect way to get me out of my superiors' lives. I had endured all the obstacles thus far. Upon notification of the assignment, I saw the intent from the start. Despite being in a critical slot, I was told that I would be going. The thoughts within my mind were at peace, for I knew that God had it all under control. The scheme was clear, send him away for what you know will be a period of six months to one year. I just knew being gone for that length of time, I would not have a slot after 6 months. With all the schemes I had overcome, thus far, I knew this one would be overcome also. I was not happy, but I proceeded to go on without any fight. There were ways that I could have gotten to stay put, but the inner feeling was let the plan go through and see how the victory will come to pass.

The date arrived for me to depart and all involved were full of sad and happy emotions. It seemed like there were many weird things happening before my eyes. The subordinates saw it as an end of an era. They were not looking forward to the new era about to come. Being the type of leader I had been, I assured them that I would be back soon. These words this time were not so comforting to those concerned. It was hard for me to leave the organization that I had built from the ground up. I was gone, and word was already flowing that it was just a matter of time before I would be off the books as a part of the organization. With all that going on, I still decided to proceed on and perform my duties at the designated Temporary Duty Station. The war was about to go in full stride at the end of January 1991 and we were primed and ready to process the anticipated massive amounts of deaths predicted. It had been said that it could go as high as a million. This was not a happy setting for any of us, at this processing point we would be notifying families of their love one's death. We had received vigorous training over the first two weeks to ensure that we did our job correctly. This would prove to be the most sensitive job I had done thus far in my 10 years of military service. The task of talking to the loved ones of our fellow soldiers who had died was an awkward feeling on the inside. I had many things to reflect on while getting ready to perform the duty. I knew that two of my siblings were already deployed into battle and the other one was alert to go. I had to ponder what I would do if their name came over the phone to say they had been killed in action.

The thought process over this matter was intense and had an impact on the Personnel Administration Center and how I saw the job. However, I did not let anyone know I had loved ones in the war zone. Now that the time was upon us, the question was asked, and I had to make it known that my siblings were involved in the war zone. I was then told that I could get out of performing this duty if I wanted to. Quickly I made my decision: I would rather be nowhere else during a critical time like this. Despite the inner entwined thoughts within, I was honored to perform my assigned duties. Many left because of that very sorrow. I felt that it was my duty. The families were anxiously awaiting the calls, and I dreaded the idea of having to talk to any of these families. Meanwhile, I was poised and ready to perform my duties. The 20th of January came and the critical war started. As the few calls came in about deaths, it was clear that the death tolls were totally off course. The truth was this war going to be over before it even started. January was gone and February halfway gone when it became more obvious that the end was near. In many ways, I was happy that the total number of deaths was far under one hundred. I was very close-lipped about the fact we would probably be leaving, back to home station, in the middle of March 1991. Here it was again that another scheme was about to backfire on the lower echelon of superiors. Just as I had said, I was about to be on my way back to the loved ones of Special Forces Training Group. The subordinates of my command felt that I would not be back there in the Student Personnel Administration Center. I was excited and happy that many of the soldiers would be coming back to their homes alive.

The death toll was still under one hundred for the entire wartime period and that demonstrated the power of God. **March 15, 1991** was approaching and that was the date of my return. The vision was still on course and six months to one year had turned into a forty-five day trip. Upon my return, I showed up the faces of all my lower echelon superiors. Being that I had over come the thirty day intent to relieve letter in July 1990, made my return all the more joyous for me. I was in hostile territory, but I was willing to endure the hostility to be able to finish this final stage. I returned to my home on the weekend to spend a few days with my family, before I went to work. When I returned to the unit there was mixed emotions: My subordinates were excited that I had returned. On the other hand, the superiors saw their worst nightmare return to their dismay. Immediately, it all started once again. The mind games with the way the Student Personnel Administration Center was being run by me. The only problem was that with the addition of the E-7 being added to the organization, I could not be drastically attacked anymore. All around knew I was still in charge, yet it frustrated the command that I had a go between to shield their direct attacks. I started to tune up the shortcomings with the Student Personnel Administration Center, while my supervisors fought the battle with the superiors. As the upcoming months begin to pass by, I was poised and ready as the E-7 Promotion Selection Board was about to commence. It seemed that the chain of command was anxious to give me the evaluation reports within an 18-month period. I saw the timing as being awkward but proceeded to accept the report. My inner being said something is about to happen, yet I had no clue what it would be. With the intense hatred for me as a soldier by particular superiors in the chain of command it could be anything. With my new supervisor being an E-7, I could concentrate on the thorn in my flesh: Weight Control Program. I was not alarmed by how one said my satisfactory progress was not being made and the other stated satisfactory was being made. I just took care of what needed to be done, get the weight under control. I accomplished that over the next few months and all was set for what was now the time for me to get selected for E-7. I knew then, I would most likely leave this organization for another job position. My work was done and I was ready to leave if the time dictated. Meanwhile, there was a change in the structure of the Training Group again. There was a Support Battalion formed in mid year 1991. There was a dramatic change and it changed the way business was being established in the battalion as a whole for some superiors. The change happened around the month of August 1991. I was now concentrating on keeping myself in a presentable status when the E-7 board results were released in April 1992. I had worked hard for the past 11 and a half years and the time had come for my payoff, with the selection to E-7. I had no doubt that my administrative performance had set me up for this selection. I had served in the position of E-7 for the past 3 years with positive results. The board had convened and I was patiently waiting for the release date of the board results. The daily duties were being done with as little hassles as possible. At times it was hard to believe that the superiors had totally caged from the hostility. I had dealt with the past 3 years. The year 1991 was almost gone and I felt within, that the year 1992 would be year to fulfill my dream of E-7. I welcomed in the year 1992 and yet I was about to enter the fight of my life in the upcoming nine days.

CHAPTER XVII

THE YEARS 1989 THROUGH 1991: MOMENTS OF CHANGE

THE YEARS 1989 THROUGH 1991 had passed by and so many things had occurred. Three years of arduous hours had paid off. Through all the good times, there had been many painful moments. As I reflected in some of these moments, it gave me greater appreciation for where I stood at the present moment. A lot of things that used to concern me, did not anymore. I had a new lease on life and I really did not know why. I viewed the new Command in a new way and that was a positive to me in many ways. All the mind games that had been played over the past three years would not be played anymore. I had endured hard times to give the soldiers of this elite organization quality service. I had been ridiculed time and time again. No matter what I strived to accomplish, it always met opposition. The reflections were going through my head over and over again. I promised myself that I would start to be more tenacious than they had ever experienced before.

I thought about the relief attempt in July 1990 and that got me in a complex position. I moved on to the year of 1991 when they clearly picked me to go to the Department of the Army Casualty Branch for some six to twelve months. These two things alone had given me the inner ability to gain the new outlook on the matter as a whole. Despite the new Command, there was a feeling that the game was not over with the old one. The way the game was going I had no clue how to conclude this attitude and how it was going to play out, but I knew that, in time, I would find out. The one thing I knew for sure is that I had enough and somehow this whole matter had come to a head. I was poised and ready for head-to-head combat. In the past I was very vocal, but I promised myself that would change in the year 1992. The reflection time was over and the time for action was upon me. This was a time for change and It would all have to start within me. The year of 1992 was upon me and I was going about my daily duties in a positive state of mind. The adversities seemed to have dissipated and that made me somewhat relieved. Things could not be better than they were on the 1st through the 8th of January 1992. Then came what I labeled as the darkest day of my life, **January 9,1992**. Feeling great within about the change in the Training Group gave me a totally positive outlook on the future. The storms were few and seldom out of control. Little did I know that a storm was brewing that would shake my whole world up. That was the devastation I had to face on what I labeled as the darkest day of my life. I participated in a grueling session of Physical Training. Upon my return to the office I was confronted by one of my higher echelon superiors. I knew it could not be good when I was asked to go outside. As we both proceeded around the building, the bomb was about to be dropped on my whole world. Questions began to arise about my history in the United States Army. In an attempt to answer the questions, I could not figure out where this conversation was heading.
Then it dropped and exploded at the same time: **Quality Management Program!**

It took me a moment to figure out what those words really meant. Then it all came clear to me: I was being considered for elimination out of the United States Army. I do not know how long my pause was, but it was at that moment that I went into a deep-depressed state of mind. I got no specifics on why all this came down, so that made matters worse. The truth of the matter was that no one knew why. I was told that the paperwork was sealed. Soon the conversation came to a close and I had to go back in the office. I did not have a clue what to do, nor did I have any answers. All I knew was that I would not be selected for Sergeant First Class. **Disappointment** was not even close to what I felt at that moment. To hear someone tell you that all you have worked for so hard for is about to be lost would be devastating. Devastation is pretty much what I felt. Anger was also a part of how I felt, yet I really did not know who to be angry at. Here I was midway my twenty year career and someone was trying to ensure that was where it ended. I had two days to wait for the answer to what caused such a negative action to be thrown toward me. I just went through many scenarios of how I could survive this attack. The consequences of this act would prove to cause many setbacks in the lives of six people.
This was my sole source of income and to have it taken away would be unbearable. The hardest part of this whole matter was that I really had no one to talk to about the matter.

The burden was on me and there was no way I could tell my family. I was in the midst of a crisis and had no clue how to overcome it. Within my mind I saw and understood why the reflection period had happened some days ago. This fight was real and it was for all that I had worked so hard for. The final straw had finally caught up with me and the way out was not clear at all. I was on my third time around with this group of superiors. Despite the fact, I did not know the reason for this action, I knew that, somehow, they were a part of it. The quality of service being rendered to the soldiers was not important at all to them. **Control was all the superiors wanted.** I had proven over the past three and a half years that that would not be the case with me. The time for war was at hand and this Command was about to see a side of me they had never experienced before. This was my **vision** and **dream** they were **attacking.**

I was prepared to fight the fight of my life. Just the thought that someone would attack me like this was an abomination of all the United States Army stood for. I was a soldier and had no intention of not being one at the expense of someone's personal vengeance. The words came to mind, here we go on one of the roughest rides ever experienced by a group of superiors. **No holds barred would be the rules of engagement in this battle.** My life support system was at stake and I would hold nothing back this time. To this point, the Command had always been in my face on the defensive end of the game. Now it was time to change over, I was about to go on the offensive for the first time. For eleven and a half years I had chosen to play defense and all that was good then. Now I have been thrown a curveball from a non-curveball-throwing pitcher. It caught me asleep for just a moment, but when I awoke I wanted a change of pace. Instead of always responding, I intended to ask questions. My offensive plays were very simple: Just throw the ball right at you and see who will be able to hold their ground in the heat of battle. Now I was the quarterback and my throws were headed for one target, no way an interception could occur. I had been in practice for a long time and I knew the defensive strategy very well. The unique thing about this part of the game was that the opposing forces would be on the offensive too. They would soon find out that the new quarterback is now the captain of the team. The game was about to begin, but before it could start I needed to go and have a conversation with my top superior. This meeting proved to be the final piece of my plays for the upcoming game.

Finally, I got a chance to go see my top superior to find out what had caused me to get this Quality Management Program Letter. To add further shock to my already distraught mind, I saw the documents that placed me in the devastating predicament. Two evaluations that I had received over the past 15 months were the reason. The clarity that I was looking for was now within sight: **Personal vengeance** was the only reason this action was done. The old Command had attacked the heart of my security and quality of Life: The United States Army. They wanted it all and it seemed as though that they had it well within their grasp. I had to go and that had to be completely out of the United States Army. How awesome it was that such a viscous attack could come my way. Being that the relief letter in July 1990 did not accomplish the mission they moved on to step #2. They sent me to Casualty Branch with a 6 to 12 month departure and that diminished to Forty-five days in March 1991. Now my whole world had been shaken up and this time it was for it all. The attempts in the past did not compare to what I was about to face at this moment. Three of my superiors had designed a ruthless scheme that was implemented over a 15-month period. They had calculated their every move to the point I stood at this moment. On the surface it looked like all this requested action was valid. You need not take it at face value without looking at the vicious plan these three superiors over a 15-month period devised. They had failed in all other attempts and this one seemed to be a secure way of ridding the U.S. Army of the likes of me.

The only problem to such an endeavor was the fact I had not reached my point of departure just yet. The issue at hand was to maintain my composure in front of my subordinates. Professionalism is what I exhibited on the outside, but deep within I could not express fully in words what I really felt. At that moment I felt helpless, betrayed, and most of all totally breathless. I just had to wait and see what it was all about. So they designed what they thought to be a concrete plan: Quality Management Program. The conclusion to the whole matter was that three of my superiors were out to take my heart. I did not conform to their agenda, and therefore I was classified to be expendable. How could this be, eleven and a half years about to go down the drain because of their personal vengeance schemes. At times it all seemed to be a dream, yet I knew it was real with life altering results if approved. When the facts were presented to me it made me angry, yet it put me in a state of mind I had never been in before. That state of mind said this act of vengeance was not going to prevail. This was clearly my toughest battle to date and it was going to take all the expertise I had to overcome this adversity. The rules in the game had totally changed in that I was no longer fighting a few superiors, but the entire United States Army. Betrayal was all I could think about during these first few days. I had given the United States Army over Eleven years of my life with dedicated service rendered to soldiers, and this was my reward for it all. I strongly felt that the United States Army as a whole had caused this negative action on me. Even though I knew that three superiors had done this injustice to me, I felt the United States Army was totally responsible. I had to live with this reality daily as I strived to maintain my professionalism.

Some awkward things began to flow through my mind and most of them were not pleasant at all. Revenge entered my mind over and over again. There were three people responsible for the two evaluation reports. There was one of them who had devised this plan of using the Quality Management Program to rid the United States Army of this Mature Soldier/ Man. Clearly I had outgrown any welcome within this Training Group. The way in which I operated my administrative operation was mind-boggling to the lower echelon of superiors. I was producing great results for all parties involved. I had clearly proven that the students were allowed to train and that within itself was an outstanding accomplishment. Despite all the great results I had achieved, it did not outweigh the fact that I was not a team player. The plays were being called at the huddle and I seemed to change the play that was called.

CHAPTER XVIII

EMOTIONAL STATE OF MIND: FACING IT ALL

EMOTIONAL STATE OF MIND: The emotions within me were very unstable during this ordeal that I was facing. All that I had worked so hard for the past eleven years was about to be taken away from me in ninety days or less. I had so many thoughts going through my mind; some of them unpleasant. **Anger was flowing out of me** during the first few weeks of this conspiracy orchestrated by my superiors. To find yourself having your entire means of support for years finally taken away is not a position I would want anyone to be in. I sorted through many scenarios to try to find the cause for such an action to be initiated against me. **Racism entered my mind.** This had gone on for some 3 years and the atmosphere had clearly defined this relationship as one of conformity. I had chose to be who I was along with doing the right thing. This was the battle line to all that was happening at this moment. I had dealt with hatred face to face some 5 years ago. So I dismissed the racism as an issue at this stage of the fight. So to a degree, I threw racism out of the equation but it could not be totally excluded from the reasoning. There was a deeper reason for it all. My superiors had a problem with me, in which, they had constantly sought a solution to: How to get me **conformed to their agenda** without rebelling against their orchestrated plans to hurt young soldiers constantly. They tried the direct approach of giving lawful orders and failed. I could not leave the foundation that had been instilled in me as a young soldier.

I believed in taking care of soldiers and along with that came the responsibility of nurturing them into solid soldiers, and endure hard times of training. I did this by acting as a mentor and coaching these soldiers into a United States Army soldier. At this point in my military career, I had decided that taking care of soldiers was the central part of my career. It was that choice that started my controversy with my superiors. Due to the many confrontations that I had endured with my superiors about my soldiers, those actions made me a target for adverse actions. They had been very simple ones during the past year and a half. Yet, after receiving my Quality Management Program letter, I realized that they had been setting me up for this from the start. They had done the evaluation reports that were supposed to be the downfall of my career. This deliberate act is what upset me the most. **I really felt like acting out my frustrations at times.** Knowing that I could lose all I had worked so hard to get was wearing on my patience. Life for me had drastically changed. My family had not a clue that in a few months they could be homeless and without the stabilized life that the United States Army had offered.

The hardest part of the whole matter was that I had to deal with all these superiors who had been setting me up on a daily basis. Maintaining a high state of professionalism was very hard at times. All the odds were against me and the comments that I had received from some of my superiors did not give me much hope at all. Yet, deep within, I believed that in the end, I would prevail. The odds against me did not matter when I compared it to the vision that God had given me over eleven years ago. The evidence was there that the vision was alive, but the inner man within said, in the end, I would prevail. The eyes of many were formed on how long it would be before I was out of their lives. It all seemed to be a nightmare that would not go away. Each night that I went home, I had to see my family move about without a clue as to what was about to happen. The more I thought about the whole ordeal, the more I was determined to correct this injustice that was put into motion by my superiors. The time had come to take off the defensive mindset and move over to the quarterback position. When I walked into the huddle, there were many looks of shock. To their dismay I was ready to call my first play. I decided to call three down and cut. The three superiors were served notice and I would ensure that each of them got a chance to get the ball. The superiors devised a scheme that was being implemented since January 1990.

Throughout the period of January 1990 to December 1991, it was the intent of my lower echelon superior to rid himself or herself of me. There were three attempts during this period of time that targeted that goal. As noted in the earlier chapter, they attempted to relieve me of duties in the month of July 1990. That attempt was squandered with a strong rebuttal letter dated 25 July 1990. The second attempt occurred in January 1991, when I was selected to go to the United States Casually Branch for an estimated 12 months. This attempt folded when I returned back to the unit some 45 days later. Then another thing became clear to me. After I returned, there were major discussions about me getting another change of Rates Evaluation Report. It was during March 1991, after I returned early caused them to have to find another means of accomplishing this goal. I debated on whether or not the evaluation report met the minimum qualification. The superiors were very adamant about it being done. It was processed and that set in motion the final part of the three superiors mentioned above orchestrated final blow that placed me where I am today. This supervisor took the two evaluation reports to one of the highest echelon superiors and specifically requested that a Quality Management Program letter be initiated on me during the upcoming **Sergeant First Class Promotion Board.** This act was carried out and now here I sit on the **15th of January 1992** debating on a course of action to overcome this vicious scheme.

I began to realize that when all the dust settled, the only way to correct this injustice was to use my expertise. The injustices were clearly seen by my other superiors and that was a positive for me. It seemed as though the ones who had perpetrated this scheme were on the run since the incoming Command clearly saw their wrongdoings. That would prove to be the best ammunition that I had in fighting to continue to stay in the United States Army. The facts were clear, yet the process of correcting it up to the Department of the Army would not be an easy one.

CHAPTER XIX

THE FIGHT FOR MY LIFE - DOCUMENTING THE FACTS

THE FIGHT: The approval of my appeal would largely depend on how each part of my Chain of Command made their recommendations. I had about forty-five days to put together an appeal packet and **I was poised and ready to start the biggest fight of my military career.** Who would have believed that I would ever find myself in a fight just to be a "soldier." The shock had dissipated and it was time for action!
Day One of this fight started with the superiors reading me the letter and informing me that I had three days till the 18th of to decide what choice I would make concerning the Quality Management Program letter. The reason for my elimination was the two past Non-Commissioned Officer Evaluation Reports I had received from my present superiors. To see that letter began to open my eyes as to what had happened over the past two years. In many ways, I was not aware of what the program was all about and never expected to find myself in the midst of it. I was poised for receiving my recommendation for E-7. To my surprise, I was informed that I could be out of the Army in the next ninety days. I had three-days to decide. The decision was made immediately after receiving my first reading. The decision was fight and win. The only thing left for me was to come up with a plan of how I would achieve that goal. After going back into my superior's office and informing him of my decision, I received from him an endorsement. Looking for a sign, I got it through that endorsement alone. When I left my superior's office, I had the utmost confidence that victory was just about nine months away. I decided to leave the case alone for a few days. His endorsement of full support and a guarantee that all others would do the same gave me hope. During those few days, I was developing a professional and thorough course of action. I looked at the facts and began to break them down one by one. The whole case was centered on "Overweight". The time for implementing the plan was at hand and all were about to see the "expert at work"

The course of action was clear, discredit the whole Overweight Program the company had implemented. I had already addressed the program in a rebuttal letter dated 25 July 1990. So discrediting it would not be a hard task. I had fought this thorn in my flesh for over eleven years and thoroughly knew the regulating guidelines inside and out. I had just overthrown the entire overweight program within this same organization in 1989. This was the second time around and the stakes were much higher this time. My whole life support system was about to be depleted. Here I go with the fight of my life.

Overcoming the Conflict

Phase one of dealing with this matter was to find out what the Quality Management Program was all about. I had never encountered the program before and never dreamed I would be learning of it to save my own career. Upon inquiring of my superiors' knowledge of the program, it turned out that the news was not encouraging. I was informed that it was simply a program that got rid of soldiers with two or more deficiencies that the Selection Board felt they could not overcome. To further discourage me, I was informed that no one had ever beat the Quality Management Program with an appeal. I learned quickly that I was up against the most intense battle of my career. How in-depth this fight for my career would be was only a few days away. Despite all the negative information, I had received about the program. I felt within that there was still hope. I had all kinds of thoughts going through my head. I began to look at the documentation I had received from the Quality Management Program and it all started to sink in as to what I had to do: Discredit both of them and then all would turn into your favor.

The two areas that they were addressing were the same: "Overweight". The two documents were from the present unit in which I served. There was two consecutive Non-Commissioned Officer Evaluation Reports. The focal point of the Quality Management Program was the Weight Control Program. The Weight Control Program was one of the administrative aspects of my day-to-day operations. I had dealt thoroughly with the program and the foundation was beginning to form. The expertise that I had would have to the winning hand after all. To overcome the Quality Management Program letter, I had to show that the entire Weight Control Program was incorrect and that unproven, derogatory information had been placed on my evaluation reports. Knowing what I had to do and doing it were two opposite tasks, yet I was ready!
The first part of knowing was not hard to do. Yet, the difficulty of doing the very act of proving that the information was derogatory would be a miracle within itself. The documents had been processed over a 15-month period of time. The stage was set for my appeal to be set in motion. I knew what I had to do and the Second Phase of this task would be more intense than the first. The plan was clear within my head and now I was about to enter the stage of documentation. To get my superiors to acknowledge they were in error would not happen easily. It would have to come through a step by step process. Through this process the time would come when they realized that they had no choice, but to acknowledge through their signed documentation they were wrong.

Second Phase would be to get my superiors to understand that the information was indeed unproven derogatory information. The position with that was the two evaluators on my evaluation reports were still in the unit. They were a part of the scheme that got me into that predicament. The deliberate attack on my career was almost over in their eyes. They felt within their minds that the era had finally come to an end, it was up to me to revitalize my career. The unique thing about this whole matter was the fact that the highest group of superiors had just switched over during the past few months. They were totally aware of the shortcomings within the unit in which I served. I knew that the support would be there for the next part. The problem with my dilemma at this point was that in order for the appeal to have a fighting chance, I had to get the entire Chain of Command to buy into the fact that I was unfairly treated during this process. And that this led to my career being on the line. The question that arose in many conversations was, were you actually overweight? To hear the answer, 'yes', immediately lead them to say that my chances of winning the appeal were impossible. To the average soldier, this would have been a fatal blow. However, my eleven and a half years of experience had taught me that even though some things were true, the United States Army had rules and regulations that governed the implementation of the various United States Army programs. That was the heart of the derogatory information being placed on my evaluation reports. It all boiled down to the documentation that caused this career-ending dilemma being done in accordance with the governing regulation. Upon retrieving the documents, the superiors seemed to feel within their minds that it was all in order. They had all the weigh-ins, which clearly showed me to be overweight. They had the documentation, which showed that I was being considered for enrollment into the United States Army Weight Control Program.

In the midst of all these documents, there stood an endorsement that was the heart of my appeal. The endorsement requested that a **Health Care Provider** clear me medically to be entered into the program. Over a two-year period, there had been no such clearance administered. I prepared verification statements for my evaluators to sign. I threw the first two balls on **February 4, 1992** and they were caught with great resistance. When my superior caught the ball, I was there to receive them back with a signature. I was forceful and deliberate with what I wanted. Produce the medical clearance or sign these verification statements saying it was never done. In the end I had the signatures and snatched the balls out of my superior's hands. I knew that the balls would have to be thrown to other superiors in the upcoming days. The time was upon me to again throw the ball, it was on **February 10, 1992** that I threw it to another one of my evaluators. This time the ball was on target but the receiver tried to get out of the way. When he realized the ball had his name on it he finally caught it. I again gave the choice show me medical clearance or sign the verification statement acknowledging it was never done. Another perfect throw and catch, I again snatched the ball because I had a few more receivers to throw the ball to. After this revelation, the superiors' confidence began to fade and they started trying to do damage control. I was set and poised to go ahead and implement my appeal on the basis that I was never entered into an Army Weight Control Program and that the derogatory information contained on my evaluation reports were, in fact, unjust and unproven. The stage was set for the Third Phase of this operation: Getting the appeal on paper with the facts that proved the two statements in fact were untrue. The fact that I was overweight was not the same, for the truth came down to the point of whether proper procedures were being followed. The burden of proof was on my shoulder. It was ironic that I had already made all parties involved admit the inaccuracy of the data centered on the

Quality Management Program letter. This was the key link to what I had to do the third phase of this appeal. Now I was about to throw the ball to all involved. I went ahead and prepared the two evaluation reports, as they should have been done. The third phase would prove to be the heart of the appeal itself.

DOCUMENTING THE FACTS: The word was out that would I be gone in ninety days. As I walked throughout the battalion, you could sense my fellow soldiers being careful with their every word. Needless to say, I went about my everyday business to get in order the appeal that would save my career. The word was also out that my Top superior had declared that all injustices in this matter had better get corrected. I had already prepared memorandums that established the fact that a Health Care Provider Medical Clearance was never done after obtaining those acknowledgments from the two superiors that wrote the derogatory statements, I was well on my way to getting this injustice corrected. Those had offered me help within my Chain of Command, but this was one challenge that I felt the need to totally handle on my own. During the phase, the facts were being established that the data contained on both evaluation reports was false and should never have been orchestrated on the reports. The whole demeanor on the faces of my superiors who saw me walking in and out the door suddenly began to realize that the departure was not going to happen without a major fight until the end. I was forceful and to the point. Now that I had the two initiators of the unproven derogatory information admitting they were wrong in writing, the time had come to move on to the Phase Four: Correcting Phase.

Time was growing short to get this appeal ready for signatures. I went ahead and prepared two evaluation reports with the correct data on them. The fact that I was single- handedly getting this appeal together had all involved on pins and needles. I had the opposing forces on their heels and I was moving in for the kill. The reports were done and the time came to get the signature on the corrected reports. I had instilled the fear in them and this would prove to be an easy task. Now that I had obtained the signatures, I processed them through the Personnel Service Center on the course to of correcting the injustice. The process was one-third of the way done. I knew within myself that after establishing the past injustices, the time had come to establish what the state of my current weight was at this time. The time had come for me to get me evaluation report due to a change of supervisor. Everything seemed to be falling into place for me. The report was done and it rated that my performance of duty was outstanding, my weight was well and in order with the standards. It also stated that I had passed my Annual Physical Fitness Test. So with time running out, I had to complete the puzzle. The facts had been established: The date on the two documents were incorrect and had been corrected with signatures and the current Evaluation Report clearly showed that I was totally in compliance with the Army Weight Control Standards. The feeling within me was full of joy and disappointment at the same time. I was full of joy because everything was falling into place in such a short period of time, yet, I was disappointed that I had allowed this data to go up in the first place. A lot of self-evaluation had taken place during the passing months. The revelations were coming clear to me: Start taking care of injustices when they happen and avoid having to handle them when your career is on the line. I also realized that even thought I had intentions of helping others, I really had fell short of that mark when it came to taking care of myself.

I was truly good at telling the Chain of Command what was right and wrong and that was pretty much as far as I went. There was not that sense of urgency to ensure that the higher echelon of the Chain of Command knew what was going on. That caused the lower echelon Chain of Command to do what they really did not want to do: tell the truth and correct the gross mistakes made. It all flowed back to the fact I had been a defensive player, defending, instead of an offensive player, attacking! Through this ordeal my function for the next 8 and a half years became very clear: be the absolute expert and attack the chain of commands in their everyday acts of aggression out of character with regulatory guidelines. Somehow I started to see this final act of aggression by my three superiors as a complete wake up call to me as soldier and most of all a leader. Now the time had come to complete the puzzle by having the entire Chain of Command acknowledge that an injustice had been done. The appeal packet was complete with two corrected evaluation reports, incorrect evaluation reports and an endorsement that clearly outlined that this whole matter was totally erroneous. The endorsement was not long, but got the message across that a grave injustice had been done. As the appeal packet made its way through the Chain of Command, the message was clear that there would be no ninety- day game plan for me.

As it reached the first Superior in the Chain of Command, the time was set for the others to follow. He made it absolutely clear that this act of vengeance should have never occurred. He also acknowledged that there were major discrepancies in the entire Weight Control Program. It was this endorsement alone that set the stage for my career to continue in the United States Army. As it flowed through the next two levels, the tone was the same as the first one. It was clear that this would prove to be one of the most eventful appeals of all time. The mood seemed to be more positive than they were when this ordeal started some 45 days ago. The time around the entire organization had completely changed. My attitude had greatly improved as this appeal packet came to pass. I could clearly see the hand of God at work through the whole process. Now this process was about to come to an end. The packet was complete and mailed off to the Standby Advisory Board for review. I knew that the chances of this packet being disapproved were naught. I had used expertise to correct an injustice that should have never occurred. The thought that came to mind was that so many soldiers in the past were not so lucky to possess the expertise that I had on my side. I made a commitment even before this part was complete: That all soldiers get to the information needed to alleviate injustices from occurring to them. I realized that this one life altering events would change many lives forever. The great thing about life is that when you find yourself in a difficult position, make sure that you know whom the expert is that can get you back straight. It just so happened that in this matter, I was the expert and that enabled me to overcome the adversity to the point that all involved acknowledged the injustice that had been done. The jeopardy of my career was about to be corrected. All that was left to do was maintain my professionalism andlism and ta of soldiers. I had to give praise to my God for keeping the vision alive. Talive.. The my faith had been tested like never before with a strong desire to hold onto something I had worked hard to obtain.

CHAPTER XX

TIME FAST APPROACHING FULL OF ANXIETIES - PATIENCE IN DEMAND

THE TIME was fast approaching for me to receive an answer to my appeal. It had been three months and no answer had been received. By that time, I was in full motion taking care of soldiers. The thoughts of having to stop during that in the next few months were unthinkable. My faith was and active and I knew I would prevail. There was not much talking going on within the organization about the whole matter. The month of June was here and the feeling in the air was that the answer would be coming down soon. I was still doing what I had a passion for taking care of soldiers. Then there was a revelation given that revealed that my appeal had been approved. I saw that the tone of the three superiors was far from jubilant and that they knew good news was about to come my way.

The mood had taken a dramatic change towards the end of June 1992. Knowing how the system worked, I knew I could not yet be notified until the paper work came through the proper channels. Within my heart, I knew it was approved. Then it came and all of them knew that I would not be going anywhere soon.

JUBILATION OF TRUIMPH

PRCE-RP-Q (AOJK-GP0FL/12 Mar 92) (601- 280b) 5th end
MSG WARD/JY/DSN 699-3704

Subject: Appeal of DA Imposed Bar to re-enlistment Under the Qualities Management Program (Enlisted Qualities Early Separation Program)

RE: Staff Sergeant (E6) Isom, Ronnie, 000-00-0000
Commander, U.S. Army Enlisted Records and Evaluation Center, (USAEREC), Fort Benjamin Harrison Indiana. 46249-5301

For Commander, XVIII Airborne Corps and Fort Bragg, ATTN: AFZA-AG-RI, Fort Bragg, North Carolina 28307-5000

1. The appeal of the DA imposed bar to re-enlistment pertaining to the above-named soldier, after careful review by a recent DA Standby Advisory Board, was approved.

2. Removal of this bar does not preclude future imposition of local or DA imposed bars to re-enlistment should the soldiers record so warrant.

3. In accordance with AR 640-2-1, remove all references to the bar from DA Forms 2A and 2-1. This correspondence will be filled IAW AR 640-10
By Order of the Secretary of the Army
Encl.
wd all encl.
CF:
TAPC-EPM-A (75B)

To say that there was jubilation in the air was far from the truth. All of my superiors, except those who had aided me in the appeal process were highly disappointed. Regardless of how they felt, I was ecstatic that my awesome God had came through again. Another vicious scheme had come to a devastating conclusion for my opposing forces. This victory was unlike any of the others in that gave me the boost I needed to start a new era within my arsenal of handling day to day problems within my military career. To have taken on the entire Command from the bottom to the top of the Department of the Army was beyond reason. Over a six-month period, I had endured the hardship of having my military career on the line. The tenacity and professionalism that I had employed during this time frame had strengthened my faith. No matter how awesome the future attacks from the opposing forces would be, they all would decay through my faith in God. Here it was twelve years in the United States Army and I moved up to another level in maturity. Without a shadow of a doubt I believe in what I believed and I was delivered to never allow myself to get in the situation I just came out of. The war games were not over and immediately it all started to heat up.

August and September were rough months in the Command. The fact that I was still in the United States Army was more than many of my superiors could bear. The smallest of things seemed to make them upset and that became the constant way of life for me in the Command. The man that most saw as just a "Black Man" had used the system to his advantage. In the end, he won and that made them very upset. I knew my time would not be long, for it would soon come to an end. I could not stay in this Command any longer due to the victory obtained two months ago. I had out grown my welcome in the Command where I started the dynasty. The thought of departing the dynasty was very emotional. I really did not want to leave, yet the handwriting was on the wall: You have got to go. During the month of September, all actions turned toward the direction of departure. It was all beginning to sink within my mind, your work here is done. The dynasty would last forever and ever. I had started it and it would always be a part of me. No one would ever know the organization as I knew it. The foundation was in my head and I vowed to never release it all to anyone. At the close of September, I was just waiting for the cue to leave. October came and I was given a chance of going out and finding me a job. I was not shocked, for the end was already realized some two months ago. I was supposed to be clearing out of the United States Army and to make matters worse was the fact that I proclaimed victory from the start. My arrogance as they saw it was more than they could bear. I chose not to fight the request because it had been confirmed that my time was up. My life was forever changed and would never be the same anymore. The conflict that tried to take all I had worked so hard to attain, had failed. I was finally on my way out of the Special Forces Training Group. **The man was about to leave, but the legacy would live forever.** The valuable lesson that I learned through the past four years and two months was how to be patient in the midst of adversity.

PATIENCE was the key to success in getting any task accomplished to its fullness. I had to lean on many witnesses of my past, to be able to lay aside all things that would lead me to impatience. I had to pay close attention to all the obstacles had would cause me to lose sight of maintaining total professionalism. With patience I was able to go from source to source and get the injustices corrected. I encountered many criticisms/abuses during my quest to ensure that the right thing was done when this matter was over. The hope that I had within me was unbelievable and allowed me to be of good spirits in the midst of a nasty decision. It took all that I had within me to be patient in the midst of evil pressing on every side. I knew that the patience would allow me to prevail because I had met the requirements set forth by the United States Army.

The whole key to my success in receiving the promise that had been given over 10 years ago, patience had to prevail. The intense pressure was taking its toll on me and I knew that it would take all the drive within me to press on. I had to allow the system to work its perfect course so that the conclusion would be perfect and complete. To the amazement of all my civilian employees, it looked to those, that there was no doubt in my heart that I would prevail. I knew within the inside of their minds they were hoping for the impossible. The track record of my appeal being approved was very dim. It did not matter what kind of soldier I was, this was clearly a chance at vengeance on the part of my superiors. I had to go home on a daily basis and portray the fact that all was well. The truth is that I knew that my God would allow me to prevail because of the promise he had made to me in the beginning. It was just hard to see how he was going to work this situation out. I could see him at work as I proceeded to get the necessary documents I needed to win my case. Each person I went to just stated they would do what they had to correct the misrepresentations on the two evaluations in question.

Over the next 45 days, I had to change the defensive nature I had displayed for so many years and let the documents come to me with patience. I could see my whole nature changing as this process proceeded on. The desire to make known all the facts I knew to all had elevated. I had learned the value of not giving my opposition ammunition to take me down. For years I had fought battles that ended up hurting me, due to the fact that I wanted to educate whomever I was addressing. The greatest thing about this new attitude was that my ears became more attentive to what was being said to and around me. The listening over this period of time taught me: That a person who listens and speaks slowly will have an effective message when his words are spoken. My spoken words became much shorter, yet sharper to the point of the matter. As the deadline grew near, it seemed like things were not moving fast enough, and I had to take many deep breaths and let my God see the process through. The packet was finally forwarded up to the Department of the Army for consideration. To the surprise of many of my superiors, the packet had strong recommendations for approval within my entire chain of command. The patience level had to really come forward at this time, because all eyes were on me for my reaction during the upcoming days. I made up in my mind that I was going to work and act in accordance with the fact that I one day would indeed retire from this United States Army. I stayed on top of my administrative duties and with all the other encounters coming from the church arena, I had to stay strong. I desired that when the decision was overturned, it would not need anything or anyone to doubt its validity. The fact that I had poured over 11 years of my life made it important tome. I did not want any favors to be called in, for it was justice that I desired to prevail. The fact that a few of my superiors saw a need to attack my family and I somewhat made this injustice more intense.

Wow, God is still in control and his glorious power still at work in my life. In the end, patience prevailed and all saw that God's would prevail. Thus, ends the tour of duty in the Special Forces Training Group.

CHAPTER XXI

TIME TO MOVE ON: 112 SIGNAL BATTALION

112 SIGNAL: The year was 1994, and it had been a rough road in the new battalion I had been assigned to. Since October 1992, I had been reassigned from the battalion where the elimination from the service contemplated. The work ethic in the battalion took on a new meaning. I was no longer in charge of my Personnel Administration Center, and this made me have to go through a massive readjustment. The Administrative actions were being accomplished on a daily basis, but the handling of soldiers' affairs by the unit was shaky. It was hard for me to just sit back and see injustices being administered to soldier after soldier. The sad part about it was the fact that the soldiers were ignorant of what was wrongly being done to them. The one part of the military that caused me much pain and grief was the level of administrative knowledge that the Non-Commissioned Officer possessed. When your leaders are not aware of their rights, then their soldiers are left out there for the kill.

The Army has many educational programs to make soldiers aware of the various guidelines. Yet, they find little time to directly educate soldiers on critical administrative matters. When you have soldier after soldier lose rank and money over incidents that were made up by leaders or the whole story was never told it bothered me deeply. It was disheartening as I began to inquire on various soldiers why their rank was taken. The fact that I was the type of Non-Commissioned Officer that wasn't afraid to speak up when wrong was being done. The fact of the matter is that the main reason why I, a Non-Commissioned Officer, received so much hostility from my superiors was due to my outspokenness. I felt that I was obligated to advise all of my superiors of the correct ways of carrying out the various administrative actions. The more I began to speak out, the more frustrated my chain of command became.

I could never understand how Army ethics were being carried out in the vision I had of a level playing field, never appeared. It assured me that time after time the flow of information was unbalanced when it came to the soldiers. The fact that their acts continued to happen made me analyze the way I would do business in the future. I made a vow to ensure that the soldier got the information needed to level out the playing field. This did not go well with my superiors. To have them start treating me in a negative manner sent a clear regard that I was heading for trouble. Despite knowing that trouble was ahead, I continued to inform the soldiers of their rights. My evaluation from my superiors clearly demonstrated their disapproval of my techniques. I always managed to concentrate on one area on my evaluation to ensure that I at least had one excellent rating. The recognition for my performance of duty was never totally recognized. It was disheartening, yet I always managed to continue to strive for excellence. I found my self in the midst of inquiry brought against me when I recommended my soldier for an Article 15. The charge that levied against me was totally unfair. To have one of my subordinates threaten a Non-Commissioned Officer and feel they should get away with it was unreal. Needless to say, the soldier got a slap in the face, and I was somewhat acquitted of the allegations.

It was not surprising that about a month later I came down on orders to Fort Lewis, WA. It did not take a genius to realize that the chain of command had requested the move. The thorn in my military career came about because the breakdown of a vision. It was time to get my evaluation report, and for some reason or another, my rates began to make a big issue about me weighing in. The fact that he wanted to weigh in was not the real issue. It was all personnel, and two went and informed my superior that despite the result of my weigh-in, was it should not. The weigh-in was accomplished and the results were personally given to me. The fact that I had presented to the superiors was validated and put on the record. The decision made by my superior in my military career. The result was unfair to me as I moved to **Fort Lewis, WA.** I know that there was a **Sergeant First Class Promotion Board** convening during my transition. I did not know whether or not that evaluation report would make it there in time. The covering of the board was **June 1994**. That was a day that I saw my dream of my military career being fulfilled. Little did I know that the very next day I would find myself in my immediate supervisor's office being told that my duty performance was well below standard. This was shocking in many ways, yet I wondered why it was happening.

CHAPTER XXII

DREAM AND VISION MEETS TOUGH RESISTANCE/OPPOSITION

When I arrived in the unit, I could see that things had the potential to get out of hand. In our field the Army has a tendency to Reclassify soldiers from the Combat Military Occupational Specialties to the Administrative fields when they can no longer function in their specialty.. Here I was dealing with a Infantry Soldier, who had that maturity seeded deep within. He was a Sergeant First Class and I was a Staff Sergeant. Our Leadership styles were as different as day and night. The bottom line is that he was in charge. During the months of June 1994 through August 1994 all was well. We had our differences, yet we managed to function together. I was deep within my sixth year of leading with the Special Forces Community. It had taken its toll on me in many ways. I had to learn to survive and little did I know that trouble was on the way. September 15, 1994 was the day that brought the first part of the Dream and Vision full circle. Sergeant First Class Promotion Board to the grade of E7 selected me. Wow!!! I was excited and jubilated. I noticed that my chain of command did not exhibit that same jubilation. Then all of a sudden it hit me: Being that I had just PCS'd under the orders of the United States Army Special Operations Command (USASOC), I was locked in for 4 years. Herein lied the problem, the current E7 would have to leave and I would ultimately be in charge of Battalion's Personnel Administration Center. I saw in that moment the kitchen overheating with no relief in sight. The thought of this "Black Man" was being in charge did not sit well at all. In a moment, it started all over again, yet I was still elated that I was selected to the grade of E7.

September 16, 1994 came and the attack soon started. I was counseled and all the good work done over the past three months had taken a turn for the worst. How could this blatant attack to go unnoticed as a discriminatory act against a black soldier about to excel in words. I gave a solid response to the counseling and proceeded to perform my duties. The one thing that I knew was that it was up to me to lose my promotable status. I had to make a choice on that day: Fight to be in charge as I should rightfully be or stay true to the Dream and Vision with God as the leader and it lead to more negative acts by the chain of command. The little acts done during the next two and a half months showed me that the command was fully set on getting me out of their hair. I was not deterred as I was in my earlier years and I was focused on their every move waiting for my opportunity to attack. December 1994 arrives and my Supervisor sets into motion what he saw to be this final blow to get me out of the command. It grew to be named the "USR Sabotage". During conversations, I had made it known that I did not like doing the Unit Status Report (USR). These conversations evidently made my supervisor feel that I did not know how to do it. Soon he presented the facts to me that he would be in training during the time the report needed to be prepared. I was supposed to do it and I gladly accepted the tasking. During the first few days that I was preparing the report, I noticed that my superior was not attending class. When I presented the report to him for review, he found a few errors and we discussed them. His plan was backfiring and then the sabotage took effect. He had instructed the soldiers I had typing the report to do whatever they had to do, so that I would not be able to complete the report.

So over the next few days this soldier told lies to me. Finally, he told me that the whole report had been lost off the computer and I sent him to higher headquarters to get another copy of the program. The soldier could not take it anymore and told of the scam. It was then for the first time realized by me what was going on. The superior had done the report and had it on his desk. All my soldiers knew of this scam and were afraid to tell me because they thought I would lose it. I performed an investigation and established all the facts and lo and behold the attack moved to another level: "Relief of Cause". My Senior Supervisor called me into the office and informed me that he was relieving me of my duties. This revelation set me off, coupled with the fact I had been set up for failure with the "USR Sabotage". The lines had been drawn and I was not about to let these actions go unexposed. I knew deep within that the entire chain of command condoned the actions being performed. I documented it all and presented it through the immediate chain of command. All I kept hearing was he was wrong, but he has the right to relieve you. I took it to higher headquarters and they wrote it off as "Personality Conflicts". I finally took it to the home station headquarters' Inspector General Team and the final results were adverse: The Relief for Cause Report was still processed with conviction. My supervisor was immediately placed on order to Hawaii. Everyone involved knew that racism and discrimination was in full affect, but the actions taken were done as a compromise to admitting truth. I would call it using the system to solve an issue without admitting the real cause of the issue. I was moved up to higher headquarters in January 1995. The attacks still did not stop by the previous chain of command. I was supposed to go to a sister Battalion and take over in the upcoming months and that was not taken well by the previous chain. The new Battalion was told about my relief for cause and the top leader of the Battalion made it known that he did not want me in his battalion. Here in March 1995 came the turning point of my military career. I could still take the Battalion and walk into a lion's den or I could get a fresh start that was being offered by the home station: Fort Bragg, North Carolina. I chose the latter. The deal was that I would be sent to 5th Corp as a quality soldier who was selected for the grade of E7 who needed a job. Headquarters would make contact with the new command. The guidance given to my present Chain of Command was that any talk of this Relief for Cause to anyone would result in legal actions being taken against the guilty party. I agreed with the standards for this transition and had one last act to perform before I departed. I met with the two people who relieved me and left them with these departing words: If I hear anything about the actions you all wrongfully did, I will formally file an Equal Opportunity Complaint on you." The look in their eyes displayed: that they knew I was serious as I departed the United States Army Special Operations Command.

CHAPTER XXIII

TIME TO ATTACK RACISM HEAD TO HEAD

Command Support Group, there I was in the midst of another E7 battle. This time I was going to meet the attack head on and aggressively. I had taken all I was going to take from these vicious attacks. The clear conspiracy that was designed to eliminate the Sergeant First Class (E-7) stripe from ever being pinned on me. I saw this as clear racism, and that is how I proceeded to deal with the whole matter. I had listened to my superior degrade me on several occasions, and all I saw in his eyes was hatred. It seemed that he hated to even have me in his presence. I did not hold him in high regards as a supervisor. Time and time again he tried to attack my credibility. I had just come off a bad situation where I got relieved some six months ago. The personality conflict had aroused thc inner fight within me. I was not going to allow anyone else to get in the way of my vision and dream. I was not a pleasant person to be around at this time, if you were on the opposing force's team. I just wanted to take them all on at one time. I started documenting it all, and that would prove to be detrimental for those involved. To call someone a racist on paper was an awesome step for me. At this point, I was not only ready, but I was willing to take it to the top of the **Equal Opportunity Ladder**. I had the ammunition to get careers altered, but that was not my goal. I just wanted to be free from the madness and get back to taking care of soldiers. Some things were beginning to become clearer to me: I was too involved with the people I took care of on a daily basis. The genuine concern that I continually displayed was somehow the center point of my adversity. The concern was embedded within my walk of life. It always went back to my growing up days: no matter how much we siblings fought, there was always a bond there that made us close in a lot of ways. I never thought that the heart of the United States Army would prove to cause me so much anxiety.

Taking care of soldiers is one of the most critical aspects of the United States Army Corp. The values that some of my fellow soldiers refused to share those that were most interesting to me. I could not alter who I was, and that continually led me to adverse actions with my counterparts. The focus on many administrative abilities was almost non-existent. How sad and depressing it was for me to be a top-notch performer, yet always having to fight off attacks from the opposition. I had grown weary after some 15 years of fighting the good fight. At times, I wondered where I would get the strength to get up and press forward to the completion of the dream and vision. My emotional state of mind was asking at times how much can one take in this profession. The words give up entered my mind, yet the inner being said you are almost there. Just allow the dream and vision to work itself out. Instead of going straight to the top with the complaint, I just took the low road that would allow me to exit this potential catastrophe. I knew it was just a matter of time before I had the Sergeant First Class (E-7) stripe on my shoulder and how much of an eye opener that

would that be for those who were awaiting my departure from the Sergeant First Class (E-7) list all together.
Tiredness had overcome me, and it was beginning to show in my attitude at times. I would find myself saying and doing things that were out of character for what I really stood for. The bitterness was rooted within me, and the time had come for it to rear its ugly head. The image that I was portraying at this time was not who, what and why I entered the United States Army. Who I was, what I stood for and why I was here seemed to be taking new meanings. The inner me was really on the rise during this time, and I was not a pleasant person to be around. The pressure had mounted to an all time high, and I just wanted to look at anything or anyone that got in my way. The case was filed though the immediate Chain of Command via the Affirmative Action Leader. All of a sudden, you saw damage control at its best. Everybody was concerned about his or her self-image. To think they were concerned about me was a gross understatement. Yet they knew that this matter would prove to be damaging to the command as a whole. Finally, I was told that I would be moved to another unit and no evaluations would be done. In the midst of all the anger and frustration that was going on within me, I took a deep breath and saw a light. This light was shining bright, and it had placed me in the center of it. All around the light were people who desired to know truth and justice. As they heard it come from my lips it made their day a better one. Their situations did not really change, but the concern and genuine care made all the difference. It was at that point that a transformation within me occurred: I finally knew what it was all about. Staying true to you, no matter what. Being who you are, no matter what. Standing up for what you believed in, no matter what. It did not really matter if things changed. What mattered was the fact that you did your part to facilitate change. I had my new unit of assignment and I had gone through a transformation that would transition me from the ranks of Junior Non-commissioned Officer to that of Senior Non-commissioned Officer. I clearly saw why many did not want me at that level: because the difference that you can make there could be dramatic to many lives. I was not welcomed because I brought something to the label that many did not care about: a genuine concern about people as individuals. Individuality was the key to the whole transformation. I first had to realize that I was an individual that had a lot to offer to the world as a whole. All in the world will not receive what I had to offer and that was the reality of life. Conformation was another word that was key to my transformation: to walk the easy road of life you had to confess to what was happening at that moment. Therein was where the choice for me became clear: be an individual and the world conformation would prove to be of no value in your day to day dealing in life. As I prepared to go to my new unit in July 1995, I had started to implement this new way of life: being ME and defining me to individuals as an individual.

The great thing about this transformation is that for the first time in my life I started to feel inner peace within about whom I was. At least I had a clue about why I was here at this place at this time: to import a part of me in individuals around me. The impact of that on the individual's life would depend on the individual. But no matter how it affected them, they knew that they had seen and experienced me in their lives. My Junior Leadership years were about to come to an end, and this new era I was about to enter would prove to be the "Defining Moment" of my whole military career as a whole. After some three and a half years after I was told to leave the United States Army, I knew why: I was an individual that was willing to share with all that came my way. All the things that used to matter did not anymore and despite all the adversities I had faced in my life, I finally got a key ingredient: Understanding. When you get that, nothing is the same anymore. All that I have ever been through has come full circle with this understanding. It took the few months in this Command Support Group to bring that understanding to me. Now the time had come for me to depart the Junior Years and move forward into the Senior Years as ME! Wow!

CHAPTER XXIV

UNDERSTANDING IT ALL: EXPERIENCES

UNDERSTANDING IT ALL: The revelation that came to me was so clear and gave me the answer that I had been searching for over fifteen years. I had allowed the events over these years to lead me into a deep state of anger. This anger had gotten so deeply rooted within, that I had become someone other than myself. Each event that had happened, dating all the way back to basic training, had fed the anger to the inner part of me. At first, it was just me who would have to deal with the affects of this anger. However, further down the road, came my wife and kids. By the year of 1985, the foundation for the anger had been established through many negatives that put me into a defensive state of mind. Once I was on the defense, it was easier to feed the anger. The opposing forces were the offense and they continually threw me curve balls unexpectedly. As each of the balls would come, I would move into a deeper state of anger and that caused many frustrations in all aspects of my already hectic life. The ball that really hit home in the early years was the Article 15 of 1984. The system seemed to have let me down. Yet, in retrospect, it was the anger I exhibited that allowed this action to commence in that direction. I was determined to get my point across no matter what. Therefore, when the dust settled, I still had not made my point due to anger that was exhibited during the ordeal. The Article 15 was administered. I served the punishment with anger deeply rooted within. That put me in the defensive mode again and would lead me to Germany for the second time. There, the curve ball was degradation of my seniority within the battalion. By my supervisor placing an unqualified soldier in charge, sent me into a deeper state of anger and brought resentment into the picture. For the next eighteen months, that very anger and resentment took me further from who I really was, and started giving me a phony identity through my many defensive moves. My focus was on the negative acts, and that only fed the anger and resentment daily within. The inner abilities that I had within me were neglected due to the focus being on a Non-Commissioned Officer choosing to do the wrong thing. The valuable time lost during this time frame was full of lost opportunities for me to focus my attention on taking care of soldiers.

Here I was in the midst of:

The Land of Lost Identities

At some point in time past, we all had an identity within ourselves. This identity is the very thing that made each of us unique. It is known as, "the time of originality". This is what we stand for and the very reason why we live. Through the years, many of us have lost that unique identity through various reasons. Some have chosen to flow with the flow and seem to get along with all, yet are not close to any of them. The word confidence, integrity, and character do not exist in these individuals. Next, come those

who choose to live a life of trickery and deceit. Within this crowd, there is much deception that causes much grief to all that come in contact with them. They are very opinionated. However, when the message is passed to the source, they said nothing. It all came from the other source. The end result of this is total destruction for that other source. How ironic is the fact that both parties talked, yet only one paid for it all: the other source. Moving on, next come those who move around life with no clue of what is happening around them. Within this group comes a lot of trickling, cymbal noises. They feel they are making valid points, yet their understanding of the whole situation is confusion. From this group, come loud noises with no weight or positive influence at all. This group works solely off ignorance. Many will follow at first, but soon will grow to steer away from this group all together.
Now, *let's move to those who align themselves with their enemies, yet always fall back* on those in whom they can depend. While things are going well, they choose to ignore their dependable friends. Yet, when all things go haywire they say these words: "Let me have a word with you!" Within their minds, they feel that they have the right to ignore those who are their friends and expect them to come to their aid without any hesitation. When told something that would benefit them from their friends, it is ignored with a negative resistance. Yet, in the end, when their enemy overrules them, they come again with, "Let me have a word with you."

Now, let us look at the group that only concerns themselves with themselves. Within this group, comes nothing but poison. Destruction comes to all those who gets in the *way of this group having their way. They find one way to bring those who can effect* their lives under their control. There are no secrets or confidentiality in this group. They will reveal your whole life story if you don't aid them in having their way. There are no limits to how far this group will go to have their way. They will spread their poison to all that pass their way. Finally, there is the group who constantly strives for perfection in all their endeavors. Yet, they are far from perfect. The work ethic is very intense, yet when it comes to speaking their minds, the intensity subsides. The end result within this group is a hardworking group that will find their response to pressure far short than how they perform their daily duties. The conclusion to all of the above is that you will constantly find yourself in the midst of a lot of lost identities. No matter how hard you strive to maintain your sanity in this environment, the fact that the lost identities are in full effect yields total confusion. How sad it is to see so many people who were born with unique identities, lose them due to the inability to allow themselves to be who they really are. So as you see these actions on a daily basis, consider the fact that these are those who have given up who they are to join the Land of Lost Identities.

Conclusion: The only sanity that you can achieve in an environment of this magnitude is to be who you are: YOU! When you are who you are, the groups of lost identities never gain the upper hand because of your originality. So continue to strive to be who you are, and life in the midst of lost identities will be ENLIGHTENING; full of new revelation daily. After this span of time had passed, the tide began to turn in the year of 1987. I knew within myself that I did not want to stay in this land of lost identities. Coming out of it would not be easy, in the least. Yet, I was determined to work my way back to where I was; however, that person I really did not know at this time. For the first time I was in the right position: A position of service. I still had the anger and resentment and that had to be dealt with to give a total quality service to soldiers. Everything was falling into place, or so I thought at that moment in time. I was promoted to the grade of Staff Sergeant/E6, and that proved to be a high positive in a miserable environment. The past six years had made me someone who was not really I. The next eighteen months would prove to be somewhat different. I was taking care of soldiers, yet I added a new attitude to my personality: "**Arrogance**". This addition caused me another set of miseries. It led me into many battles with the Command's superiors. The past eighteen months had not yielded the tension I was experiencing now. It became clear to me that positions of power led to misery when you speak what you believe to be right. To add arrogance to that equation could prove to be deadly. Positives did come out of the last eighteen months. I took care of soldiers, I learned a lot about dealing with a group of superiors at one time, and I learned that the position I finally got a chance to hold was the heart of the Personnel Service Center.

Now to the negatives I created within myself from a confrontational environment with my superiors and the addition of arrogance to my set of attitudes. In the midst of all of the many positives I accomplished in taking care of soldiers, the greatest loss was I had developed no relationship with the soldiers I took care of daily. It seemed like I was just going through the motions. My attention was so diverted toward the Command and its desire to have its way that I did not see beyond the actions that the soldiers requested. Behind those requests were human beings who had lots to offer as a person. As I meditated on that very fact, I prepared to leave Germany. I left for Fort Bragg, NC, with a very ambitious mind and attitude to develop relationships with soldiers I serviced daily. Through those relationships, maybe I could find my true identity along with helping others to do the same. I felt like I could take the whole world on at the same time. I came in full force and created a dynasty: Student Personnel Administration Center. That did not sit well with the superiors. I was so set on correcting my issue with developing relationships, that I neglected to stop my opposing forces from orchestrating a vicious plan to rid themselves of my presence in the United States Army. My shortfall was that I allowed negative/critical data that almost caused me my career to go on my Official Military Personnel File. It forced me to be the absolute expert and display an awesome faith in God.

I had been going around ensuring that everybody else was taken care of and totally neglected myself. During this ordeal, something became clear to me: You cannot help others in the United States Army, if you are not around. I had to learn how to prevent such vicious acts from elevating to this level anymore. I could not alleviate them altogether, but I could minimize their affect on me at the lowest level. Seducement was the key to accomplishing this mission. In the end, I got a new lease on life through my Quality Management Program (QMP) appeal being approved. That new lease on life brought about another change of attitude: The time had come to leave the defensive mode and cross over to the offensive mode. Time would prove that this transition would not be an easy one.

This caused me some hard times during the next two and a half years. My time in the Dynasty Group came to an end. I moved on to the Battalion of Signals. Over the two years I was there, the grueling transition began to take form. I was doing what I was supposed to do at a very optical level. During a United States Army Special Operations Command's inspection, I managed to come up with six commendable/great ratings. Yet, the most important thing that I did was start individual relationships with fellow soldiers. By doing this, I began to define myself as the person I really was: me. The value of others defining me began to diminish. The schemes that came my way were met head-on and were never allowed to put me in a career-ending predicament. I was the absolute expert, and I had many character witnesses who would counter the negative picture of me as a soldier painted by some of my superiors.

The complete package was coming together for me as a soldier. The opposition was still up to the same old trickery, but something else began to happen around me. Subordinate soldiers began to fall in love with me as a leader. The heart of my purpose had come to the forefront: Teaching, Coaching, and Acting as a Mentor through service. Through that service, I started to be surrounded by soldiers who would start fighting those who tried to hurt me. The supervisors/superiors started to take note of how the soldiers were starting to defend my character. I learned that as you take care of soldiers, they will take care of you. The bonds that I was making on a daily basis would follow me wherever I would travel in life. My time at Fort Bragg, NC, was about to come to an end. I had developed individual relationships that would follow me throughout the rest of my lifetime. How rewarding it was to start seeing a little bit of who I really was as a person. I knew I was on track to leaving the land of the lost identities. It was true. As I decided to be me, many enlightening things were revealed to me daily. I started to see people for who they really were and this alone gave me the knowledge and wisdom of how I needed to deal with each of them individually. The word "individually" has grown to be the key to success in my daily walk of life in the United States Army. I saw my time in Fort Bragg, NC begin to come to a close, and that move would turn out to be the most important move of my life to date in the United States Army.

CHAPTER XXV

NEW ERA - THE SENIOR YEARS: MATURITY

THE SENIOR YEARS: After a grueling three-month battle with the superiors of the Command Support Group, I made my way to the land of the Fire Mission. I was drained but still full of determination to excel. I felt that the past three months was the start of my transition from the junior level to the senior level years. July 1995 was the month and year, and I was poised and ready to fulfill the dream and vision from the Lord. My old superior had given an ultimatum to superior officer to take my weight control packet down to my current unit. It was an endorsement in the action to that directive: No action. Meanwhile, I was on course to taking corrective action to position me to gain the final leg of my promotion status: Sergeant First Class (E-7). Upon my arrival to the unit I performed the following tasks within the first 30 days: passed the Annual Physical Fitness Test and met the weight standard without the test being administered. The time was set in the month of August 1995 and how important that would prove to be in my promotion. The promotion for the month of September 1995 came down and, lo and behold, my sequence number was there. Finally, the dream and vision had come full circle in the grade arena. Jubilation was in the air as I saw that day come and go. Through all of that Jubilation, there were some anxieties that did not allow me to make great this jubilant event just yet. I was not going to allow anyone to take it away from me. The fact that I did not have it pinned on the effective date of the promotion was not a problem to me. The truth of the matter was as, of September 1, 1995, I was, in fact, a Sergeant First Class (E-7).

So, there it would be that several months would go by that only I knew I was a Senior Non-Commissioned Officer. Unbeknown to all around me, I was slowly learning the rules of the new ball game. The understanding level was constantly becoming more and more clear. I know not what I had to do: "BE ME!" Here I had been through struggle after struggle without a clue that it was all about ME. All those around me were different, because of the simple fact that I was different. How could such a thing be, someone would ask. Well when I looked within myself, I saw that the past 15 years had been years of conditioning for such a time as this. All that I needed to win this battle was the knowledge on the inside of me. The key to my future success was not to allow any actions to penetrate within, to the point where I stopped being ME. I was smart, intelligent, and most of all a soldier who could make a difference in many lives. I felt renewed within with the knowledge that I had to be the greatest me there could be. Senior years are here and I must move on down the road and stamp the final mark on my United States Army Career!

Here I was a young, black man, on the verge of entering a world that would change my whole life, as I knew it, as a soldier. The Senior Non-Commissioned Officer Field was unique within itself. All the rules changed, and nothing was the same anymore.

The level of intensity in which I had exemplified during the past fifteen years was nothing compared to the road I would travel for the next five to nine years. It seemed as though I had arisen from the dead with a new life and the opposition knew it was just a matter of time. I was forceful and energetic in standing up for what I believed in. I knew that the level of responsibility had increased by leaps and bounds. I was now in the position where I could affect and enact changes. I was the power force behind soldiers when it came to their administrative matters as a Senior Non-Commissioned Officer. I no longer had to sit in the background awaiting word from my superior, for it was I who was the superior now. The time had come for me to fulfill the promises I made during the year.
The voice that would be heard by the many soldiers became one of the most inspirational voices to hear. There was hope, and soldiers knew I stood for the right thing. My soldiers loved working for me, and knew I had their best interest at heart. I was not one that you wanted to go home with, but I was one that you wanted on your team. I believed in the hard right approach. Stand for what was right, even if all involved opposed you. Be your own person when you spoke, and make it known.

Life in the Field Artillery was an experience in many ways. The most grueling test of what I was made of, both physically and mentally, was the twenty-five mile road march. It was September 8, 1995, and I knew I was about to tread unknown territory. I was pumped for the march and knew that adrenaline would get me partially through it. What would happen after then, no one knew. I had protein, and that was a plus when we started the march. The first 11 miles was the adrenaline march, but it was the last fourteen that took me to the limits of my physical and mental abilities. The protein no longer worked, and the uphill battle was taking a toll on my body. I continued to put one foot in front of the other, despite the facts that the steps got shorter and shorter. Fifteen miles was where I had to do a physical and mental check. The physical check said that this is it, I cannot go another step. The mental check said, I am all you got, and now you have got to dig deep within to be able to make it to the finish line. The word 'quit' was not an option for me. I knew that it would be costly to my career to have to face my superiors without completing this twenty-five mile Ruck March. I stepped and stepped and found myself two miles away from the finish line. Quitting was still not an option, yet pain and agony was found in every step I took toward the ultimate goal. I told my fellow soldiers to press forward, and I would see them at the end. It was taking all within me to press forward. Drive, intestinal fortitude, instincts, and whatever I could muster from within was keeping me moving.

Finally, I saw the light, and to my amazement there was an array of leaders awaiting us as we walked across the line. The Battalion Commander told me that I was now a Field Artilleryman. This unit has a sentimental value to me in that it was the first unit that I was totally in charge of my administrative operations. The battles were many, but I took them on one by one and corrected them. The key point was clear to me was that no one ever doubted my expertise in the administrative field. The central problem that opposing forces had with me as a soldier was, I do not come on the bandwagon of railroading soldiers. I spent arduous hours talking to young soldiers, advising them on how to keep them out of trouble. The Good-Old-Boy click was not for me. I knew that my life in the military would be an easier one if I did, but that was not the road I chose to travel.

Being an individual was more important to me in that it was what drove me to speak to the issues as an individual. It did not matter whose side my opinion agreed with, I spoke it, as I knew it from within. Many soldiers benefited from the opinions I spoke. The criticalness of the position I was in was powerful. The guidance that I offered would affect soldiers and the lives of families. The fact that I had experienced the earlier attacks on my military career, family, and life made me the more sensitive to these sort of attacks on others. The difference you can make as a Senior Personnel Administrative Sergeant can be both diverse and stimulating. I watched many soldiers lose their money, rank, and careers over soundless acts. Who stands up for you when facing adversities is more essential than right or wrong? Guilt and innocence does not serve as the final right of administering judicial action/punishment. The lack of administrative knowledge of very sensitive matters has been costly to many soldiers. They go through legal action after legal action and do not have a clue that grave injustices are being done time after time. That is where I came in, to ensure that the playing field was level. I was the absolute expert and now I was the Top-Enlisted soldier in charge of the Personnel Administrative Center. WOW!

CHAPTER XXVI

HARDSHIP ON THE WAY: KOREA

KOREA: Upon my arrival in Korea, I was already on the ropes. I knew that I was in a deep battle with the thorn in my flesh: The Weight Control Program. I was well overweight and did not have a clue to what I would do in the upcoming year. As I started inprocessing, I did enter the office for a weigh-in. I was found to be thirty-three pounds overweight and it was noised around the whole group. There seemed to be a great concern among the group of whether I could function within the group. I knew weight control program or not I was going to function as the Personnel Sergeant of the Group. All my subordinate soldiers knew about my weight problem. Privacy within the military really does not exist at times. All eyes were focused on me and being a Senior Non-Commissioned officer with 16 years plus, I knew how to handle that. The outgoing supervisor made a living noising around the fact that I was fat. It was also rumored I would not be staying in the Group because of my weight. There was about a 56-day transition period then I had the shop to myself. The first order of business was to get the subordinates within my office focused on what I was all about. I started off with the fact I was on the weight control program. I made it clear to them that being on the weight control program, would have no affect on me performing on the job. I made it clear to them that I was here to take care of soldiers and not be scared of the command. I then began to establish the rules and guidelines on how things were to be done. After the meeting was over it was clearly understood that I was about business. I commenced to do what I do best, take care of soldiers. The command found out quickly that I was not to be taunted because I was overweight. I clearly let them know it was a personal problem that I would deal with. When it came to being about military business it was not open to discussion.

When it came to my weight control problem, that was not open to the world. I was a sticker on "need to know" basis. I had the same problem with my old superiors. Yet, this time it was different. I was more seasoned in using my brain and mind. The outburst had leveled out and the constant arguing was over. I had to deal with the highest ranked group of superiors, I've ever dealt with before. The greatest test to date was before me. I knew this was going to be the roughest year of my military career so far. It was time for me to be tested on my ability to be a total professional. The time for maturity had arrived and I was gamed for the test. The expertise that I had accumulated over the years made me an invaluable asset to the soldiers of this Group. To compound the problem of working with the highest-ranked group of superiors, I was on a hardship tour. Korea was the hardest tour that I had to deal with. I did not have access to my family and I could not just get up and see them. As time passed by, I started developing a plan of action to combat the wrongdoings within the group administratively. During the two-month transition, I noticed a lot of errors in how administrative actions were being carried out. Some of them were totally out of touch with the regulatory guidelines. The treatment being given to certain soldiers was close to the point of being illegal. I began to deal with them one at a time. The command began to make it clear that I was starting trouble. I had promised myself that once I became a senior non-commissioned officer, I would dedicate my final years to training young soldiers how to do the right thing, and survive while doing it.

I was chosen to be a Platoon Sergeant despite the fact that I did not want to do it. I strongly thought it would interfere in the full performance of my primary job. I was given it anyway. I immediately called the platoon together and let them know where I was coming from. I knew this would be a challenge, but I was gamed. Meanwhile, I was still confronted with the overweight program. I started weighing in monthly and noticing irregularities. Being seasoned in how to handle different situations, I just observed and took notes. It was important to be professional about all I did. I knew that timing was also important. To attack the program while I was in it would not be effective. It would be looked upon as me trying to get myself out of trouble. The interactions with my superiors were steaming. I was constantly in heated discussions with them all. I did not have any reservations about standing up for the soldiers of the group. I was developing enemies and for once it did not matter. I had fifty-six soldiers in the platoon that depended on me to fight for them. I also handled the administration for all the soldiers within the group. The Platoon Sergeant position made my life more complete. I had never experienced this in over sixteen years. I found myself in meetings with superiors from other platoons who outranked me. The issues that arose made them angry with me, because as a Platoon Sergeant, I had the same authority. Hanging out with the big boys began to be fun. I was in position to help soldiers in two capacities.

About six months into the tour, it became a critical time in my military career. I had been in the Weight Control Program for six months and it was time for my six-month weigh-in. Rumor had it that word was out that if I did not make it during the six month weigh-in, I would be considered for separation from service. I was still holding my peace on the irregularities of the program itself. The weigh-in was unbelievable. I did not know how it happened, but when it was all said and done; I had not made the weight, but I was in the body fat standard. I clearly saw it as a miracle and nothing could be said by me. I was happy and excited about the news. I left the weigh-in station smiling inside. The results of the test were brought in the office and just thrown on the desk. Again, my privacy was not allowed. Now that this challenge was over, I was more motivated to drive on toward the end of my tour. The timing was approaching to attack the weight program as a whole. I was no longer in it and I could proceed. It was a few months before Higher Headquarters would be coming to inspect the group. It had been announced there would be a group inspection done. This was my opening to get the irregularities corrected. During the groups' inspection, I used one of my subordinate soldiers to conduct the inspection. I prepared a comprehensive inspection sheet and it was set up to evaluate the Weight Control Program in-depth. The fact that even soldiers had been in the program off errors made this inspection important. The inspection was conducted and of course the results were failure. During the out-briefing, I made it clear the only way to correct all the irregularities was to start all over again. The implications of this inspection were that all soldiers were never enrolled into a Army Weight Control Program. This was good news for all that had been wrongly enrolled in the program. Here it was again that the thorn in my flesh had been overturned due to the improper implication of the program.

Meanwhile, many other things were happening with the group. We had just went through a change of command and it was better for me. To the superiors of the Command it was a living nightmare. They could not figure their new superior out and this made their lives a living hell. I saw a superior that wanted change and had a plan to implement it. I just knew from all the changes I had been through before that I had to continue to do the things I had been doing. I had to go through a few adjustments, but when you follow the regulatory guidelines, there is not much need for change. I have never seen a command turned upside down by one man, as this group was. Coming from the trenches of the United States Army I knew what was going on. The group was in frenzy and all I was doing was taking care of soldiers and the Command. I had been established as one of the premier Non-commissioned Officers in the group. The hardship tour was being dealt with through genuine bonding between fellow soldiers. It was nearing nine months and it was time to go home and visit my family. I knew that in my absence, the soldiers would be open for attack. Thus I assured them I would be back. The trip to see my family was great and I returned to Korea for my final 100 days. I was pumped and ready to meet all challenges head on. Upon my return, the wheel started reeling to a conclusion. I was on my last leg as a Platoon Sergeant and was in the ready rooms for the final battle. As the tenth month rolled around, I was up for another physical fitness test and that was not something I was looking forward to. I had pains in my shoulders and I did not know how I would fare with the thorn in my flesh.

The superiors were highly upset with the tenacity I used as I performed my job. The round was coming to an end and I had to complete what I had started. On one occasion, I found myself in an intense conversation with the second highest superior in the group. The situation had come to a head and we both needed a release. I stood face to face with the superior and professionally relayed my feelings on the matter at hand. There was an attempt to pull rank, but the nature of the discussion was centered on expertise. I was being the expert and the superior was looking out for himself. There were no wrongs or rights, just two stubborn soldiers having a healthy debate. It was that debate they made me realize my maturity as a soldier. I had come full circle from being a stubborn, junior soldier into the senior Non-commissioned Officer who could stand toe-to-toe with the best. Although my superior did not care for what I was saying we had the utmost respect for each other. That was more than I could say for some of the other superiors I had the distinct pleasure of dealing with. There was times when I had to flat-out refused the instructions I was given. The legality of something in question, I would not place my career on the line. The refusal to carry out various orders would lead to some saying I was disrespectful, but the truth of the matter is I had an obligation to be the expert. Being the expert in my field made me responsible for the administrative actions that went on within the group. I knew my job well and that allowed me to say no to orders on many occasions. Superiors knowing they could not get me for disrespect would look for alternative ways to get back at me.

I arrived at the company to take the physical fitness test and passed it. I was not so fortunate on the weigh-in. It was found that I exceeded the body fat standards again. Some of my superiors got excited thinking this was my second time in the weight control program. Ignorance was the sum of their happiness. The entire weight program had been overturned during the group's inspection. The superior who would be responsible for reading me into the program had no care for me at all. He had bought into the notion that I thought that I was bigger than he was. In our discussion he made it clear to me that he should be reading my rights to be chaptered. He acknowledges that because of some technicalities, he could not, the reasons were already known to me. I held my peace because none of what was being said had an affect on me. He ensured me that this time I would be entered into the Weight Control Program properly. He would personally monitor it. I was given the proper documentation for a medical evaluation. An appointment was made and I did attend it. I gave blood and did all the other things that needed to be accomplished. I was called to be informed that I would be called back to have it completed. This was about the ten and a half months of my tour. I continued to do my job. Documents were done signifying to the group that I was already entered into the program. Being the mature soldier I was, I just let the ordeal play itself out. My superior was responsible for rating me and did not care for me as a soldier. The biggest problem I had was the rapport I had with the soldiers of the group. It seemed to have a dramatic affect on her, when she saw the rapport I had with them.

We did not agree on any of the administrative matters. I would tell her on many occasions, I would not do what I was being asked to do. The fact still remained that I was the expert. Despite the fact that we did not get along, I was professionally taking care of my superiors. It was known that when things went wrong, the expert would get most of the blame. The Weight Control Program was her ace in the hole. She knew that I would be leaving in about forty days and that a NCO-ER would be required. What a way, she thought, I could get back at him for all the headaches he caused me. I knew I would have deal with that when the time came. My replacement had arrived and it was time for me to transition. One of the hardest, but most rewarding tours was about to come to an end. I had thoroughly grown up to total maturity as a soldier. I was about to leave the big boys and had survived with my sanity. The platoon I had grown to cherish was about to be released to someone else. I had all kinds of emotions within. How could I leave those I had grown attached to as soldiers? How could I not leave and go join my family who I had been away from for 2 years and 5 months? How could I retain my emotions within during the last days of my tour? I was relieved, yet depressed about it all being over. To move from childhood as a soldier to adulthood was very revealing. The time had come to depart the country of Korea. The change of responsibility had taken place between the new supervisor and me. I was no longer in charge of the platoon or the Groups' Personnel Administrative Center. The war was coming to an end. I waited for the last thing I needed from the Command: my NCO-ER. I did not expect an award form my superiors. There was no sleep lost over that. I had not been able to reach the doctor to complete the needed paperwork. I knew that my final confrontation would be with my evaluation report. I was poised and ready; just waiting to be released.

I was poised to go out as I had came into the Group: The expert that shook up all the erroneous tactics. I finally received my evaluation report and it was one of the worst reports I had ever seen. It was not the worst because of what was written on it, but because of what was not on it. It was blank except for the weight control entry being there. I had just been through an inspection where I received four commendable ratings and I knew that would be added to the final copy. I was fully aware that I was not in a Weight Control Program. I went to my superior and passed along the information and placed her in a state of shock. She was very upset and started making phone calls to the superior who enrolled me I would been entered into the program over 40 days ago. After extensive questions with the Commander, she should have found out that indeed I was not in any Weight Control Program. The dilemma that was then left, was what to input on the evaluation report. As the expert, I informed her she must put that I meet the standards. This placed her in an up-raged state. She proceeded to check out the validity of what I said only to come to the conclusion that I was completely right. Here, again, within a matter of months, I had escaped the snare of the thorn in my flesh: weight control. I began to wonder how many lives I had before the "thorn in my flesh" would overtake me. The superiors were looking at each other to blame, but the fact of the matter was no one could be blamed.

The reason why so many errors were made was because the help and guidance of the expert was ignored. It had become common practice that whatever advice I gave my superiors, they would do the opposite. In the end, they would have to throw out most of their actions because of the neglect to follow the guidance of the expert. I would give them what they needed, but because of their personal opinion of me, they ignored all I said. They reminded me of myself in my immature days as a soldier. In my junior years, I would not listen, and I caused myself a lot of sleepless nights. I clearly understood what using the brain and mind meant. I did not get my evaluation report before I left Korea, but I was counseled and assumed it would be corrected. I signed my portion with the correct date and proceeded to say farewell to the group and Korea.

My farewell was very emotional for all that attended. The one thing I had instilled in my soldiers was how to say farewell in style. The feast we had for some of our outgoing soldiers was called the Bomb. The group was there, and then one of the most intriguing things happened. The top superiors of the group graced my farewell with his presence. The shock that showed in my superiors' eye was astonishing. He came in and ate, talked with me a while and then left. I saw it as an appreciation of respect for me as a soldier. I was in the trenches and I knew what it took to survive. Person after person said their words and touched my heart. One of the most intriguing words that was said was when one of my young Non-Commissioned Officers stated that I, as a soldier, would fight for them with no regard for my own rank. That was a statement of high regard, but it signified to me right away that I had better take note and change the way I fought for others and start saving some of my fight within for me.

I held the tears back and then it was time for me to speak. I acknowledged my superiors and then sentiments for what the year meant to me. For in the end, all people will remember is the moments. I expressed an urge to not leave yet a greater desire to see the family I had missed for 2 ½ years. The tour that helped me grow as a soldier was over. Good Bye Korea, you will never be forgotten as the land where I grew up as a soldier.

Bonds had been made that would live forever. Subordinate soldiers had seen their future careers set up for success grade moves. We all were better off because of the many moments we had shared together during one of the hardest tours in the United States Army. Almost eighteen years complete and now I find myself heading toward the level of the "Air Assault".

CHAPTER XXVII

HOME OF THE AIR ASSAULT: FT. CAMPBELL KY

The time was fast approaching for the unit to go to the National Training Center. To see myself in an Infantry Battalion was not where I really wanted to be. To top that off, I was assigned to the land of Air Assault, Fort Campbell, KY. The two things I had declared I never wanted to be a part of was thrust upon me at the same time. Just coming off a hardship tour did not make me excited about my present situation. Upon my arrival to this duty station, I made an attempt to get assigned to the Personnel Service Center. That request fell on deaf ears thus leading me in the land of Infantrymen. I knew somehow that this was not going to be a smooth ride at all. Knowing that this was the land of Air Assault gave me another obstacle to deal with. Word was out that all would be Air Assault Qualified. From the start, I had no intention of going to the school and the Command did not like that at all. The ground rules had been set early during this tour of duty. Being a seasoned Senior Non-Commissioned Officer gave me the upper hand on this situation. The command knew they had their hands full and were definitely trying to come up with a course of action. I was still on the offense and had no intention of giving up the ball. The administrative situation was ugly to say the least. Yet, I did not see that as a major problem because I knew in a short period of time all that would cease. To add to the confusion, there was an upcoming inspection of the entire Personnel Administration Center. I just observed as the preparations were being made and I knew that the results would not be pretty. After it was all over, the news was not good at all. Being that I was new, I was sought for the solution to the problem. I gave the answer and it was not welcomed: More Command Involvement. My superior came back to me to correct me, proclaiming that he was constantly involved. I further took it to a level that opened his eyes in two ways. I clarified my statement to the point that he understood that it would take more than him to set this problem in order. The second thing that he understood was that all the rules had changed because I was I charge now. I assured all involved that all areas that failed would be dramatically changed over the next 90 days. I had made the promise that I would be a mentor and coach for the rest of my time in the United States Army. The subordinates were looking for leadership and I was their chosen leader. I saw their hunger and I welcomed the challenge to feed them. The command was curious as to who I was and their curiosity would not be satisfied for some time to come. I refused to lay out my offensive scheme to this and that would lead them down a road of constant expectations and curiosity. Adventure was what I had chosen to make my last days in the United States Army.

May 1998 brought about a change that would further enlighten me on all I've dealt with during the past 18 years. I was chosen to attend the Equal Opportunity Course. The course was only two weeks in duration and it would prove to feel like a lifetime for various reasons. The Command was still riveting from the Command Inspections. The higher-echelon superiors searching for answers to their many problems. One of them got very angry with me entering the Equal Opportunity Course. One day during a discussion, he expressed his issues and I listened. I realized that I as the king was in and that is the very way I would be for my entire duration of duty at this command. The course was starting to bring some interesting facts out about the inner thoughts of soldiers in the United States Army. We all thought ourselves to not be a racist, prejudice and capable of discriminating against another person. How revealing this course would prove to be. Just a simple question began to get the whole class aroused and that set off the discussion that would bring the entire class down to earth. The truth is; our opinions alone-breathed racism, prejudices, and discrimination from within each of us. Then something odd began to happen. We all started to admit that these three things were a part of our lives. Two words stood out at that moment: Thoughts and actions. Our thoughts, which led to our opinions, were the source of the racism, prejudices, and discrimination to life. The course had done something to me that eighteen years had failed to do: Show me who I could be in thoughts versus who I was through my actions of the past. All the thoughts that I had revealed through this class thus far was a part of me and yet no one knew them through the actions I had demonstrated over the past 18 years. Racism was an active part within my thought process, but I had not shown these racist thoughts outwardly through my actions. Prejudices were many and yet my actions showed that because of the organizations I was a part of I did not act all of them out. Discrimination was really the heart of our thoughts and yet actions again had prevailed in my duration of duty thus far in my career. In many ways I was relieved, but then it was time to move on to the heart of why we were at the Equal Opportunity Course: To help alleviate there who goes beyond the thought process into the "Action Phase". At that point in the class there was a renewed focus to how serious this class was to the United States Army. Another thing that came to life at this point was the many racist acts each of us had seen during our military career. We were introduced to a type of racism that we would be responsible for searching out Hidden Racism. There in was the problem that each of us faced at this point of the class. Looking beyond the acts of those in positions of power and seek out their motives. Motives would grow to be a powerful word in the Equal Opportunity. This task would not be an easy one in that many people were very cleaver in their racist acts. That started me to looking back to my early days when I saw the Racial Profile Breakdown of the United States Army in various commands. It led me to review some of my experiences with that profile. It was through these reflections that I welcomed the opportunity to make a difference in my latter days of service. It also gave me some enlightenment on why there was so much resistance to me completing this course. I stood up for what I believed to be correct and right. This fact alone scared some of the superiors in the Command. Finally, we had completed the Equal Opportunity Course and each was sent out to employ the valuable training received over the past two weeks. I had experienced another life-altering event in my life as a United States Army Soldier. I understood these words racism, prejudice, and discrimination like never before. In my present command, I had already seen some of those very acts performed. My goal was to try and illuminate them to the light. My popularity greatly diminished after I graduated. The time had come for me to start focusing on the Personnel Administrative Center of this elite Infantry Battalion. The problems were many, yet the solution was simple: Start doing the right thing now and over time they will be corrected. The morale of the soldiers was down due to a lack of guidance. I called all of them together and gave them a better outlook on the whole situation. I could tell by their expressions that there was a renewed hope for brighter days ahead. I started to build a solid team that consisted of a variety of players. Each of them had shortcomings, yet they made great contribution to the mission as a whole. The challenge to me was to take a group of misfits and make them into a viable working team of soldiers. This would not be easy, but I knew it would come in time. Many were close to being chaptered out of the United States Army. All those pending actions went to rest upon my arrival. This was going to be my last tour of duty in the United States Army. I was going to get it all right this time.

All the experiences of the past told me that the time had come to shine as all the adversities come my way one by one. Being in the land of Infantry, I knew I would see it all again. The results this time would be totally different. With the Equal Opportunity Course behind me I was poised and ready to make it all work this time. It was not long before the Weight Control Program crept up on me again. I had seen it many times before so this time I was going to make it through with the minimal heartaches. The one thing that had finally come my way was the 17-year, 9-month anniversary. It was this that had secured me to my retirement baring some stupid mistake by me. I had made my share of them in the past, but this time I would not be denied. They placed me in the program and again failed to perform the critical Health Care Provider's clearance to be placed in the Program. It was their program and they smartly took it out of my control and gave it to the medical section. I had learned how to allow the responsibility to stay where it belonged. Each month when they called, I would weigh-in and that was a hit-and-miss process. Meanwhile, I was taking care of soldiers with career saving service by making them the expert on matters that could hurt them down the road. I was also aiding the Command on advice of how to take some of those soldiers' careers away from them. Both sides heard both positives and negatives, they really did not want to hear. Many times what I had to say was against the Command's wishes, but I was only an advisor. On some occasions, I would ask them what was their guidance after I advised them. A peculiar question would come from one of my lower echelon superiors: "Is it legal or not?" How ironic the words I had spoken to him over the past few months had began to sink in: "Sir, I will do what you instruct me to do as long as I do not have to sign. Also, when I am asked by higher headquarters if I advised you on this matter, I will say, 'yes', and that you chose to do it anyway." I was making him responsible for his decision and left no room for him to blame me down the road. Wow, it was working!

CHAPTER XXVIII

LOOKING BACK - BREAKDOWN UNITED STATES ARMY (RACIAL PROFILE)

UNITED STATES ARMY (Racial Profile): The racial profile of the United States Army was very interesting in some of the Battalions in which I served. I found it to be surprising when I actually started looking at them on the Quarterly Equal Opportunity Reports. It was shocking to learn that the ratio of Whites to Blacks was 7:1. To have these numbers staring you in the face had to make you wonder about the equality of it all. That breakdown became more troubling when you went to the breakdown of the Officer Corps. This is the Command Central of the Military. Usually, there are about 40 officers assigned to a Battalion. Out of these 40 officers, you might have three Blacks and about 35 Whites. To further magnify the profile, none of the three would be in a Command Position. They usually worked on the Staff. The Command decision in my military career had been made 97% of the time by White officers in Command Positions. Just the numbers themselves relayed the message that there is no equality. To imply that all White officers were racist is not the case. What is the case, is that the decisions being made by our Command Officers were majority made by White officers. You have to understand how fair decisions cannot be made when there is not fair representation. I have had twenty years' experience being close to where the decisions are made. There were many instances when the decisions were bias to race. I did not see it as racism, but it was to those involved.

To have the needs of a wide-based variety of races under your control and have no knowledge of each race's tendencies can lead to a vast majority of racist decisions. The decision does not make the person a racist, but it has the same effect. To not have input from all represented races can be detrimental to the underrepresented races.
The clear understanding is that there are more races than Black and White. As a Black man, I will focus on the two because they set the tone. The facts are clear and cannot be disputed. To have the majority of your Command Position led by the White world leads to decisions being made by the White world. You are the product of the environment you grew up in. At the start of my military career in 1980, I was not a long way from 1968. It was in that year that Blacks received the right to vote. Just that fact, alone, speaks of the domination the Whites have enjoyed over the years. To say that 12 years later, it all changed would be a lie and deceitful way of thinking. I believe that great lengths were being taken by the United States Army to ensure fairness. (Yet, the decisions were made in the trenches and out of ignorance, many had no clue what was going on.) I saw what was heard during many distributions of punishment under the Uniform Code of Military Justice. The system itself is a fair one, but the implementations of it were the source of the problem. I was always looking at statistics and they showed the trend of how unfair the system was.
The unique thing about Command decisions is that they do not keep up with their

profiles. It could be said that some of the Whites in Command were not aware of the recent decisions because of not keeping profiles by race. Some of them had mended their ways after the profile was shown to them. (The profile clearly showed that the end result of punishment by race was inconsistent. The same officers that delivered the totally different punishments combated those trying to use the fact that the extenuating circumstances were different.) This does not substantiate the inconsistencies. It must be known that this inconsistency is not the total fault of the Command decisions. It starts with the Lower Leadership positions. That is where the foundation is set. The Leaders of the Officer Corps had the inner need to carry out the desires of their superior officers in Command. The choices of a young officer were limited when they first came on active duty. They have one Officer Evaluation that will determine their length of time on active duty. They are in the Bind of Doing. Their survival depends on whether or not they are team players. Their knowledge does not dictate whether they will stay on board. The implementation of the Command's Philosophies plays a large role. I have personally seen the officer's struggle and they are awesome. Seeing these changes around me made it so that I never wanted to serve the United States Army as a Black man.

The few experiences I had with Black officers have not been a pretty sight. Some of them disheartened me a lot when I looked at our already unfair racist profile. The twenty years of service that I have given my country yielded zero Black Battalion Commanders; two Battalion Executive Officers (XO) and two Company Commanders. To see these over a twenty year period is startling and shocking. It left me wondering what it was that made it so difficult for our Black officers to get in these Command Positions. The answer could only be found in the ones who are making the decisions of who goes in these positions. When you understand that the majority of the decision numbers are White, it will lead to what I alluded to earlier. A lot of racist decisions were made, again, this does not make the decision- makers racist, but the same effect is achieved. You have to understand that over the years standards have been established and they continue. Despite the fact that Blacks have been accepted to the military openly, we have had to fight a lot of hidden racism. The hidden racism is not commanded by the United States Army, yet it equals the same result when it is being exercised. To prove this would be very hard, yet deep within my heart, I believe it is there. The saddest part about this hidden racism is that the acts are compiled behind the scenes and carried out in the open by the Black race.
How shocking it was to see a Black soldier being used to carry out the hidden racism of another race. You see, the belief is that if I get the Blacks to do it to the Blacks themselves, then racism is hard to be identified. How far from the truth that statement was when you saw it first hand. These acts are mostly carried out at the company level and they are covered up by all involved.

Blacks have been well represented in the position of First Sergeant and Platoon Sergeants within my last seven years in the Army. At first, this made me feel good until I began to see what was really going on behind the scene. My last seven years in the United States Army was when I began to see things clearer than ever before. They were always there, but my attention to others was directed as I ignorantly fought my battles with my mouth.

The one thing that got me in trouble as a Black soldier was the abundance of mouth and lack of use of brain and mind in my early years. I would lay all my cards on the table. That is how I would combat the intentions of my opposing forces when a majority of them were White in the trenches. My belief was that if I had it disclosed by mouth, it always stopped it. Little did I know that all I was doing was causing them to come up with another plan. After the big event that tried to have my career, I woke up and started using my brain and mind. It was then that I started seeing what many have seen throughout the years: You can make all the rules and guidelines to combat racism, but you cannot change the hearts of men and women. For, it is with the heart that most of the decisions are made with in the Command positions.

CHAPTER XXIX

LOOKING BACK - THE REALITY OF HIDDEN RACISM

THE HIDDEN RACISM comes alive when you team up the races, yet only one race has the decision power. The one thing that I have never experienced was being the subordinate of a Black Company Commander and a White First Sergeant. Many consisted of a White Company Commander and a Black First Sergeant. The sight of seeing a Black First Sergeant walking alongside a White Company Commander would somehow make United States Army feel better. How far from the truth this proceeds to be for many others and Black soldiers. First hand, I have shared time and time again with these First Sergeants and listened to their frustration. Over and over again, they told of the many times they found themselves behind the Commander's office, being told who made the decisions in the company. They were disgusted with how orders were being carried out. The stories made it clear that the hidden racism was to be carried out by the Blacks in the non-command positions. You wonder why they would not stand up against it. They had families to support and had endeavors of achieving a higher rank within their military career. There are many that had an effect on their decisions to cooperate with the hidden racism. To say that all acts were carried out on Blacks would be totally untrue. Yet, to say that decisions are not made by the Command positions permanently occupied by Whites would be far from the truth.

The United States Army would not want to be on the public record stating that it had a racism problem. Yet, when you look at the numbers of Blacks and where they are positioned, it speaks for itself. Racism is alive and well in the United States Army and it is found in the decisions being made daily. Racist decisions are hard to see, yet it is there and has effected many careers over the years. One would probably ask if more Blacks were in these Command positions, would their decisions be racist. I would venture to say, yes, but not to the degree we have with Whites today. There are several reasons for that: one is the fact that they go out of their way to ensure that they are fair. Secondly, they are so thankful for being selected by the dominant White decision-making panel, that they go out their way to prove they are worthy of the nomination. Many who read this book would call me to be a racist, yet the fact remains that I never had a chance to implement it because I had no decision-making authority. So the power of racism within the United States Army comes alive with the power to make decisions. Those who have no power can only enact their racism by confronting those who have the decision-making power. This leads to the other source of hidden racism down at the lower level of soldiering. The Sergeants are another source of hidden racism. It is all the level with Blacks as well as all other represented and this is the area where the racism begins. It is at this level that taking care of soldier starts. The awesome task of taking care of soldiers is a central part where hidden racism effect soldiers from all races.

Up to this point, the power of racism has been solely in the hands of the decision-makers. Now, at this level, we move into another part of racism that affects our soldiers daily. I will call this the Active Racism. Active Racism is when you are the authority to abuse a soldier just because you can. It comes from Blacks, Whites, and other races. These acts could be seen as leadership-at-work with you beginning to observe the reason of why they are happening. There had been cases where a soldier constantly received active racism just because of where they came from as a child. There have been many that received active racism because of the color of their skin. I do not blame this on the United States Army, for you cannot change the hearts of men with rules and guidelines.

There have been three occasions that I have experienced an account of the rope being tied in 13 knots. I have had a superiors come to me as the Equal Opportunity Non-Commissioned Officer and tell me of a Black soldier's experience with a rope tied in 13 knots hanging from the barracks railings. He felt it was intended for him. I had firsthand knowledge of a Black mother calling the Battalion Commander talking about her child fearing for his life because of the White the threats he received. Is active racism alive in the United States Army? You judge for yourself.

The agenda of outside organization are alive and creative in the United States Army. To feel that you are in a gang-free United States Army is far from the truth. To feel that the White gang organizations are not alive and well in the United States Army is also far from the truth. To go farther, there are also a lot of Black gang organizations alive and active within the United States Army. To acknowledge these facts puts you halfway to solving the problems they cause. The amount of soldiers that have gang related material proves the fact that various organizations are functioning within the United States Army. Some will feel it to be shocking n active duty. I can remember in school when I would hear of people coming around with "White sheets" on. I was asked on one occasion, "What would you do?", and I simply replied, "I would run." Yet, I experienced firsthand an event dealing with the organization known as the Black Panther. The announcement was noted that this gang would be showing up at our school on a certain date. To my amazement, when that day arrived about 50% of the White students did not show up to the school. The other 50% hung close to the Blacks simulating that they were friends. The reason for mentioning this story is that the awesome display shown towards the Black Panthers coming was shocking in a way. It seemed as though the fear level was different. The organizations were the same in my eyes, yet the affect was not the same at all. I clearly got the impression that the Black Panthers were a group to be feared and the Ku Klux Klan was a group to be accepted in America.

So here we are down in the trenches where the active racism goes on daily. The active racism at this level was tentatively unbearable to watch. The fact that it was called corrective training by the activator of the active racism did no justice to the one receiving the act itself. Yet, I knew it to be a long way from what the United States Army intended to be corrective training. To take the authority that the United States Army gives you by virtue of your rank and abuse it is totally wrong. I know from experience that authority has led me to proclaim to my superiors many times that we not: not working on plantations. That was my way of letting them know that their ons.ions were close to being what I have labeled as active racism. When my white superiors would hear these words, their reaction was one of shock. The fact that I would say those words brought to reality what they were doing. You see we are a product of our environment and for many white soldiers their environment down through the years has been one of authority over the black race. Slavery was real and many of their ancestors owned slaves. Many times during my last years within the United States Army, I would see the words of racism boiling at the tips of many of my superior's lips as they saw what they call a black man being disrespectful. In my heart I could feel them saying " If only I had you a few years ago, I would show you what respect for your superiors really mean. I stood my ground on the authority that the United States Army gave all soldiers/leaders and many of my white superiors could see was a disrespectful black who lost his way through the years. The punishments I received were all centered on the fact that I would not submit to their authority. Down in the trenches almost 90% of my leadership who had authority over me were white. So when I talk of my bout with Hidden Racism it comes from my personal experiences through 20 years of living down in the trenches where the real acts of racism, discrimination and other controversial actions happens daily to anyone who does not conform to the authority in charge.

MANY OF THOSE WHO SERVE IN HIGH POSITIONS OF AUTHORITY HATES ANY INDIVIDUAL WHO DEFILES THEIR AUTHORITY REGARDLESS OF WHETHER THEY ABUSE IT OR NOT.

CHAPTER XXX

LOOKING BACK - RACISM EXPERIENCES SHARED

RACISM EXPERIENCES: As I talked with one young back soldier, as the Equal Opportunity Non-Commissioned Officer, he told me the story of how his White superior would always do demeaning things to him in front of others. He kept records of the dates and circumstances of each event. During a major exercise towards the end of my career, the White superior had led the young Black leader to another demeaning task in front of his squad. After performing, the act the young Black soldier arose and said "Sergeant, you are a racist!". He began to break down the different racist things *he had done to him in the past. The revelations of the actions brought it to life that he* was a racist in his actions and the superiors of the Command took actions to correct the problem. Here, again, is another example of active racism being enforced daily by superiors toward subordinates.

Another firsthand experience was when a White leader had formed platoon squads and had what was beheld as a White platoon. During an argument, the all-White squad was given the task of laying out items in the shade to be inspected. The squad with the Black soldiers was sent to the motor pool where it was hot. They were told to stay there until the inspector came. The allegation was found to be true. Another sign that there is active racism in effect. It was no accident that this squad was not mixed up with races. A clear example, of when a superior is using their authority to carry out *that racist decision. Another experience of active racism was during a major exercise.* There was a White superior who was told that he would be receiving a Black soldier in his platoon. He called a platoon meeting and the issue came up. While the White superior was talking, he made a comment to the only other Black in the platoon, "I know that this Black soldier will be coming to this platoon, but I will not put up with any of y'all Black actions." This was putting it mildly. The case was investigated and proven to be true. Now, the White superior was punished, but did not lose any rank. He had to attend the Equal Opportunity Course at Home Station. Here, again, active racism in the United States Army.
Also experienced on several occasions was use of the word 'Nigger'. Some were proven and the soldier punished. Yet, through all of these known cases of active racism, there are many that have never been exposed.

I remember the time I was asked to teach a class on racism. It was during the end of my 20-year career with the United States Army and I gladly accepted the task. I pondered how I would teach the class where as it was interesting, yet very much to the heart of racism. I decided to go with what I know best, telling it like it was. To start the class off, I proclaimed that we all were racist. I proclaimed that we were all prejudice. To hear me proclaiming myself a racist got the whole classes attention. I knew from there, I could go on to educate them on ways to deal with their racist attitudes. As the class wore on, I began to break down to them that the purpose of this class was to get you to acknowledge that you are a racist, at least in thoughts, and understand that the United States Army dos not want you practicing racism while on active duty. To deny that you are not is the very link to so much active racism. You see, the intent of any program is to make you aware of your problem and give you solutions to not allowing them to become a part of your professional service to the United States Army. One would say that there is no harm in participating in a KKK or Black Panther rally. On the surface, there is nothing wrong. However, when you look at the fact that you are a part of the United States Army, then everything changes. You send the wrong message: the United States Army condemns your active participation in that it allows being a master of your own desires. The whole moral of the class was stop spending valuable time trying to convince others that you are not becoming a racist. Rather spend your time acknowledging that you are with full concentration on not letting it affect the professional and quality service the United States Army has called you to render. Acknowledgment is the key to overcoming this active racism being administered by others who are in denial of being a racist.

Finally, to my personal bout with active racism. I was one Black soldier who could get rid of most of the racist attacks with my knowledge and positions I had held during my military career. Being an administrator like I was made many cautious of how they came after me in the racism area. I was very vocal and did not mind letting them know how I felt about their actions. There was only one occasion that I had to face active racism head-to-head with an internal complaint being filed. It was in the year 1995 that was a very hectic year for me as a whole. As noted in the chapter it was during the time I got selected as an E-6 promotable. I was sent to the group and saw an active racism plot on the horizon. The actions were being done along the lines of professionalism, yet I knew the racist acts of the individual. I could see the racist attitude in his actions. Every time I would get in a conversation with him, his more superior than others attitude would come in his tone of voice and the manner of the conversation. I tried to with all I had within me to deal with the problem myself. Time after time after time this became a career-threatening event. I did take action. The bottom line was the acts of racism were the fact he liked his White to White relationship he had with the out-going Sergeant. He devised a plan to get rid of me and keep her in the position. Her input in the ordeal was hidden racism, where she carried out his directions to set up and plan to demonstrate my inability to function as a Non-Commissioned Officer. I did not care to be in that type of environment, yet I was not going to let racism go without exposing it. The heart of it all was that she was in total denial of being in active Racism State. It did serve a major purpose for me and it brought to my attention that being in a superior position did not give you the right to abuse your subordinate soldiers. I was a mature 15-year old soldier and I had enough of the constant abuse that soldiers endured on a constant basis. From that day on I would fight this active racism head on. The head-to-head encounter with active racism made me realize that it was alive and well in the United States Army.

Opening eyes would be the answer to getting this problem under control. It will never be totally out of the United States Army. Denial is the only reason it is there no matter how you look at it. Racism is racism no matter what you call it. I as a Black soldier met this challenge head on. I am sure that my bout to get rid of active racism would be very active as time went by. The United States Army has guidelines and regulatory guidelines that prohibit the act of racism. It is up to you as soldiers and fellow Americans to make sure these guidelines are carried out. Regardless of your race, you have to acknowledge that you are a racist in thoughts and manners and find ways not to enact this racism in your daily dealings. Knowledge is the key to stopping hidden and active racism.

THE DISCRIMINATION AND/OR RACISM TEST"

"**How would a reasonable person be affected by certain acts**" would be a great to quantify the below actions as discrimination and/or racism?'

- Being within a platoon with an all white squad?
- Being supervised by soldiers who have less time-in-service than you have in the grade of E5
- Being told with a group of whites that the platoon is not going to put up with any of your black heritage.
- Having attacks and obstacles coming from your white supervisors daily to the point where your career within the United States Army is threatened?
- Having a 13-knot rope hanging from the window and you are the only black around?
- Having your supervisor use your white soldiers to set you up for failure in front of all your subordinates?
- Constantly hearing white supervisors telling you that you need to find your place and stay there?
- Being ordered as the only black to attend a function just to show that no discrimination or racism exists?
- Overhearing superiors asking what race the supervisors are?
- Being in a command where 13-knot ropes are left at the Charge of Quarters Desk?
- To hear a mother of a black child call and reveal that her child is afraid for his life with the knowledge of a 13-knot rope appearance within the Battalion?
- To see Chain of Command pictures of various commands over and over again with all whites in charge.
- To have a white superiors come to you at the end of their tour of duty and apologize for their actions. Admitting that they were told that this black man would be your enemy because he did not cooperate with the "click"?
- Being labeled as a Black Man just because you choose to make a stand for what is right regardless of race, color or creed.

CHAPTER XXXI

FINAL ATTACK - CONSPIRACY IN MOTION

It was a time of joy for my family and me as we went to Fort Bragg, North Carolina on the 9th of February 2001. It was the first stage of settling down for retirement. To date, I had served nineteen years and seven months. Little did I know that while I was on that mission, my superiors were hard at work to destroy it all. The plan was in motion the very day I left for Fort Bragg, NC. The intent of the actions was clearly to place a bad taste within me as I departed the United States Army. It all started at six o'clock that morning during the regular meeting of the Non-Commissioned Officers. They stated during the meeting that I did not have an approved retirement packet. They told my subordinate leader to process my retirement packet. This statement was very alarming to all in the meeting because they all knew that I had informed them that I had an approved packet. The scene shifted to the Battalion Headquarters, where they were holding the monthly Promotion Board. The same superior put Phase Two of the plan into effect when he asked one of my subordinates of my whereabouts. His answer was I was on Permissive Temporary Duty; the reply to that was "No, he is freaking not. He is freaking Absent Without Leave!" It must be understood that those present were the First Sergeants of the companies and the Command Sergeant Major of the Battalion. What an awesome revelation to be made! One of the battalion's Senior Non-Commissioned Officers had just gone Absent Without Leave after 19 years and 7 months in the United States Army!

In a matter of three hours, they had noised my name around regarding my defiance of the United States Army Regulations. The fact that they had declared me Absent Without Leave, put my whole career in jeopardy. The fact that I was about to retire, made the declaration of me, being Absent Without Leave confusing to most of the soldiers. Meanwhile, it seemed that my request for permissive temporary duty leave was gone. I had gone to great lengths to ensure that several copies of it existed. They all had mysteriously disappeared. Upon arriving at my destination, I went on to settle my family down. Thus, ending the sequence of events on 9th of February 2001. On 10th of February 2001, the actions intensified on the implementation of the Absent Without Leave theory. Two of my fellow peers were directed to go to my office and perform an inventory of all my property within. News of this event was spreading fast, despite the fact it was only in the second day of implementation. I had made a call back to the office and was well informed of the events taking place. I continued to settle my family. It seemed like the nightmare of 1991 was starting again. The difference was that I was wiser and the enemy was working off of ignorance. They really did believe that I did not have an approved retirement packet in. They really did believe that they could pull their conspiracy off due to that very fact. The repercussion of them being right could prove to be detrimental for my United States Army career and could seriously place my retirement in jeopardy. They knew that I had an approved permissive temporary duty leave form, for it was in their possession. What they did not have in their possession was my approved retirement packet and orders. Therefore, their whole case's validity stemmed on the fact that I did not have one approved.

Without an approved retirement packet, the charges were as follows; taking permissive temporary duty leave under fraudulent conditions and doing so with malicious intent to defraud the government. This is why so many of my fellow soldiers were in deep disbelief. Personnel Administration was my job and these things I knew to be true. That is what made so many believe that their allegations were untrue. The whole Command was standing in awe awaiting my return on the 22nd of February 2001. The case seemed to be in smooth sailing motion for the opposing forces. The inventory of my personal property was done and it was shipped to the Supply Room. This event performed in front of my soldiers proved to be devastating for their emotions. Their leader was some 600 miles away and they were seeing the command setting in motion a plan to destroy his whole career. They were sitting on the edge of their seats waiting for their leader to return. During my conversation with my soldier on the tenth of February, I informed him to let all my soldiers know to hold their peace and all this will be straightened out upon my return in about eight days. This ended the second day of the Final Conspiracy.

Eleventh of February 2001- Phase Three of the plan was underway when the superiors behind the actions instructed my subordinate Non-Commissioned Officer to call my home number every hour with the message that my superior wanted me to come in. Further instructions were given that after each call, call the superior with the result. Here, we see another critical part of the plan in motion. A time line being established of trying to find a soldier who was Absent Without Leave. The results were already known. The call would be made and a negative reply would be received. The ironic thing was that my subordinates were being used to establish a case against their leader. Thus, ended the events on the third day of the Final Conspiracy. The plan was in full motion after the sequence of events from the 9th of February through the 11th of February 2001. All the pieces were in place and all awaited the punishment phase. The weekend came and went and another week was upon us. The superiors started implementing the course of action to set the punishment phase into action before I returned. The 15th of February was when a clear decision was made that I would be relieved of my duties as the Personnel Sergeant of the Battalion. To further insult me as a soldier, the superiors instructed my subordinate Non Commissioned Officer to move into my office. He refused to do so in light of the things he had heard from me. It was noted in the relief letter that I had committed several violations: I had lied about having an approved retirement packet, I was on an unauthorized absence, I was frauding the government, and I was said to be in an Absent Without Leave status. Just the fact that it was being spread throughout the post that I was Absent Without Leave was stunning and awesome.

The shock of the revelation to my fellow soldiers was overwhelming, for they had no words to express their disbelief of what was being said. It seemed that the acts being talked about was not the acts, expected from a soldier they had grown to know in their daily dealings. The fact still remained that the word was out, that a Senior Non-Commissioned Officer had just abandoned a 20-year career and gave it all up.
It was all set and all that needed to happen was for the victim to return to the scene. The word victim is how I felt during the days of this outrageous assault on my career. The day had finally arrived that I was to depart from the settling of my family. It was an intense ride and the water was boiling over on the inside. It was on the 18th of February 2001, that I arrived back to the battalion. The loyalty of my soldiers had proven to be a great asset to me while I was away from the unit. I knew of all the Chain of Command's actions before I returned. This knowledge had given me the time to come up with a plan of attack that would make the conspirators look like people of vengeance, instead of the leaders they were commissioned to be.

The 19th of February 2001, the eleventh day of the Conspiracy, I was working in my office. The entire post was on a four-day weekend due to Presidents' Day being observed. My immediate supervisor came into the office and it was not long before I inquired of him about the rumors going around of my Absent Without Leave status. His face told me a lot and it was from there that the Conspiracy commenced. I assured him that all my actions during the past eleven days were in order. I proceeded to explain to him that my retirement packet was approved on the 10th of December 2000, and orders had been issued on the same date. The shock on his face was a clear signal that the ignorance of the whole scheme had been revealed. The whole direction of the Conspiracy had shifted and my supervisor was trying to take the high road. I was upset and the gist of the conversation was not pleasant. To make matters worse, after I finished letting my frustration out, my supervisor said words to this affect, "It is too nice of a day to get upset. I am going home. We will discuss this later." He departed and I knew the tide had taken a turn for the worst for my conspirators. I enjoyed the rest of my weekend and thus, came the day that I must face the initiator of the Conspiracy. During the morning meeting, there was a bold declaration made that I needed to be in the office of my supervisor today. That was not a surprise to me. Yet, I knew that the meeting would prove to be a shock into the insight of my Absent Without Leave conspirator. I had all my documentation in order and this would be the first time it was revealed. I approached the initiator and inquired of him about why he wanted to see me.

CONSPIRACY was still in motion to portray me as a Non-Commissioned Officer with no integrity. The whole foundation of my service rendered to the service was being of high integrity and trustworthiness. The actions that was being contemplated was targeting toward putting a negative mark on my career that could ultimately lead to a court martial and possible withdrawal of my retirement from the United States Army. My emotions were very high and it took all within me to hold my peace and allow this conspiracy to be handled in a professional manner. The more I meditated on the deliberate attack on my career, the more agitated I became within. I knew that there would be no repercussions, for the allegations became the documentation that cleared me of all the false allegations. It seemed as though the conspiracy had come to a halt and the air was let out of the balloon in mid-air. The case seemed so solid that I was convicted before I even had a chance to hear the charges. I was informed that I would be going to S4. During a discussion with the initiator of the Conspiracy, I was informed that the Chain of Command had expressed a strong desire to court-martial me for a list of violations that I had supposedly committed. I was accused of governmental fraud, in that I was on an unauthorized leave and that I had committed several offenses of lying that actions had been completed, which they believed were not. The plan for my relief of duty had already been set in motion and the search for a replacement was in full affect. The basis for the request was that a Senior Non-Commissioned Officer had lied about having a retirement packet approved, no orders for retirement being processed and in the process of all that he was Absent Without Leave from his unit without proper authority.

I patiently listened to all the charges and then in a flash of a moment I placed several documents in his face that changed his whole attitude. The truth was staring him in the face and he then knew he had to find an exit out of any blame for the false accusations that had been levied against me during my absence. The finger pointing immediately started and then he revealed to me that he was the only one that was fighting to keep me out of trouble. I relayed the message to him that it was about time to set the record straight and also time to let the higher Chain of Command know about the destructive attempts that was being made to destroy a soldier's career who had devoted his whole life to serving his country. I informed my superior that I was not going to report to S4 because I had done nothing wrong. I let him know that I had full intentions of going back to the battalion Personnel Administration Center and do what the Army had trained me to do: take care of soldiers. He knew within that I was not in a joking mood and that he, along with the others, was not safe from punishment for the malicious attack on my career. As I closed out the discussion with him, I again relayed words to the affect that the higher chain of command must be made aware of the type of malicious attacks being committed to soldiers who have given their time and service to preserve freedom. I was very disappointed that no one had any confidence that I was wrongly accused. Needless to say, I concluded the meeting with my superior and proceeded on with duties as the Senior Personnel Sergeant of the battalion. The key element on relieving me of my duties had just been handed a lesson in how ignorance can make you down right foolish. He knew that his contemplated attempt to demoralize me as a soldier was demolished. I did not come out and tell him, but within my heart, I knew he was the initiator. Thus, ending the confrontation on the 22nd day of February 2001. All through the rest of that day, I met soldier after soldier who proclaimed: "I knew those things being said were not true." It made me feel good to know that despite the fact the conspiracy was out to destroy my career, it ended up enhancing it in the eyes of the soldiers I had serviced on a daily basis. The joy displayed by my subordinates was overwhelming, for they had seen their leader come back and put to rest the false accusations in a matter of hours. The superiors who came up with this conspiracy were very frustrated and I knew there would be retaliation planned down the road.

Things were almost back to normal, when I encountered another one of my superiors on the 23rd of February 2001. This confrontation was more intense that the previous one I had experienced the day before. I was confronted outside the battalion area about why I was not in formation. I explained that I was in the midst of performing a battalion's Personnel Administrative Mission when my superior went off with words to this affect, "When I fire somebody, I expect it to be done." I informed him that I had no knowledge that he had fired me and I had not a clue as to what he was talking about. This made him very angry and he ordered me to come in his office right now to get this matter straight. My emotions were still riding high and suddenly something within me snapped. I told him, "Yes, it is time that we get to the bottom of this matter." Both of us were upset and there seemed to be clear sailing to a massive confrontation. His demeanor was very negative and intense in that he relayed words to me that when he says that something is going to happen it will. We took the meeting into his office and I felt like I was on the defense again with a surprising element being revealed to me; there had been no relay of the information that had been revealed to the First Sergeant during our earlier meeting days earlier. This was not surprising, but it did lead me to smile on the inside as he read me up and down about the shortcomings that I had done as a Senior Non-Commissioned Officer.

After his very powerful presentations, I went on to break down the facts as it was done before in my previous meeting. Confusion levied on his face as I continued to pile on the facts. I expressed my difficulties in trying to serve a command that did not place soldiers' needs first. I went on to elaborate on how this Command loves to treat soldiers like trash when they come to the end of their career. I was just pouring my inner feelings and would always reinforce my feelings with a reminder of the deliberate attack upon my career. He constantly tried to ignore the situation at hand, but this was my moment and I was not to be denied. The tones of our voices were high-pitched. This was the most intense meeting I had ever had with any of my superiors within this battalion. I can say that I was borderlining being disrespectful and insubordinate. I knew that the shock of my superior seeing the documentation that he was told never existed had broken his concentration and put him on the defensive. His demeanor continually changed as I made him aware of all the deliberate attacks this battalion was performing as a whole. I constantly proclaimed that I was fully prepared to take these matters as high as the 18th Airborne Corps Headquarters. I was hurt, irritated, disappointed, and downright angry at the conspiracy that this Command had set in motion against me. After about forty-five minutes of grueling discussion, cooler heads began to prevail, the tone calmed down, and the end result was that I would continue to do as I had said: work in the battalion's Personnel Administration Center.

I left the office and felt like this was the final day of the contemplated conspiracy. Little did I know that it was still in high gear. I attended to the personnel matters of the battalion. The battalion was scheduled for a personnel asset inventory to evaluate the accountability roster. Despite all of the negative attacks that were being levied upon me, I still maintained a positive attitude toward the accomplishment of my mission. We received a strong rating on the mandatory personnel asset inventory. The next phase of the mission for the day was to have an assistance team come down and give the Personnel Administration Center an assistance visit. One of my superiors came into the office and requested that the whole inspection team come into a small office with the office. He proclaimed that he had negative knowledge of the visit, but gave them some shocking instructions: "I want you to find all the negatives within this Personnel Administration Center." His logic was I couldn't fix them if I do not know them. Little did he know that I knew of his deliberate attack on me and I had already enlightened the Non-Commissioned Officer in charge. He came into my office and said words to this affect, "I have never heard anything like that in my whole career in the United States Army. I do not see how you stay here with attitudes like that against you." He promised to do a fair visit, and that he did. We received our out brief and this ended the sequence of events on the 23rd of February 2001.

During the next day, everything seemed to be going all right until I noticed a lot of my superiors going back and forth into my immediate superior's office. I could tell that there was something mischievous brewing in the pot. I heard one of them say to my supervisor, "I'll see you at the Officers' Club." It all began to come into focus. My supervisor called me in the office and said that he had a letter of concern that he wanted me to read. After reading it, I informed him that I would be writing a rebuttal statement submitted by the 25th of February 2001. After about twenty minutes' discussion, he proceeded out of the office with the copy of my decision. I knew that he was angry because he did not obtain just a signature as instructed. They all knew that if I wrote a rebuttal statement, it would again blow up their attempt to relieve of my duties.

Here, we go again. I knew that the same individuals who had tried to attack me before were at it again. I had a meeting with my soldiers and then we went home. Thus, concluding another sequence of events on the 24th of February 2001.

CHAPTER XXXII

CONCLUSION TO THE VISION 27 APRIL 2000-1735 HOURS (Final Thoughts)

The time had come for me to release the United States Army into the hands of the younger soldiers. The vision was complete and I knew that it was time to depart an organization I had served for twenty years. The joy of being in this position was awesome. A lot of reflection on how I got where I was went on daily. The thought of all the hard and rough times was unbelievable at times. The achievement of twenty years within the United States Army was a great achievement. As I started to look back on it all, it finally began to sink in that I had spent my last twenty years in a whirlwind of confusion. Yet, when all the smoke cleared, I had attained the ultimate goal: Retirement! The task of moving on was a bittersweet move. It was sweet in that the impossible had been achieved. To have heard the many superiors that proclaimed that this achievement would never be achieved made it even sweeter. Scheme after scheme had the intention of killing the vision. The fact that I had come up through the trenches also made it sweeter. The wounds within and the battles were a reminder of how rough the road was to this end result. As I looked back, I saw the Quality Management Program, which was the knockout punch, it brought some of the bitterest emotions that I felt at this moment. The questions of why it took all of that puzzled me. The many attempts to have me chaptered for being overweight along with the Final Conspiracy scheme that happened 9 months before my retirement was effective. What it all meant was that what had started out over twenty years ago as an adventure turned into a nightmare along the way. I knew that it was over, but it was only the beginning of the new era. A Man had survived the unendurable and it was a miracle within itself. I was thankful that God had enabled me to fulfill the vision he had shown me over twenty years ago. I was about to embark on the life as a Retired Civilian.

The thought of staying past twenty years was out of the question and I knew it. The dream and vision had come to an end and now it was time to move on. The last days of reflection made it all come into focus: The vision was given to enable me to drive on when the odds were all against me. In general, I spent my entire career with the odds against me. I give all the glory for this completed vision to the Almighty God. I was only the vessel that he used. Here I stand proud and tall knowing that a Man from Monticello, Florida has given twenty years of quality service to the United States Army. He faced the many hardships, yet he held on to the vision. In the end it was the vision that kept his career alive. When all said it was over the vision and dream somehow it will survive and go on. The lesson of this tour of duty in the United States Army is that: Dreamers will always win in the end as they continue to dream. The dreamer was about to depart the Armed Forces, yet the dream still lives on. The end of one dynasty will lead this Black to another. Keep your eyes and ears opened for the new dream: The Man That Took the Civilian World by Storm.

I sit here at Fort Irwin, California with these thoughts in mind. It is obviously clear that many sad events have happened in the past three months and due to those events, some resentment is locking around my heart for certain individuals. The question is not whether of not the resentment is valid, but whether or not I am going to let it find a hiding place within my heart. I must honestly say at this moment it has not and will not succeed at that attempt to lodge within my heart. Yet I only feel that it must be put to rest in the first few days that I return to Fort Campbell, KY. After doing that, it must not be ever talked about again in a resentful way. It is a positive in my life for it increased my already strong faith. I know without a shadow of a doubt that I am one of God's chosen vessels. I seek no retribution for anyone over these matters, for I know that all involved will reap what he or she sows. I see this as a farewell to the greatest Corp within the Army. NCO Corp that I have been a proud member of since the year 1982. The 18+ years of serving this United States Army has been rewarding, yet it has left some tremendous scars that will always be there to remind me that "whatever you do, it is going to cost you. Are you willing to pay the price?"

I have chosen over the past twenty years to pay the price for being that I am me! I have continuously face adversity for making that choice. The end result of all has been many pain and heartaches. I always felt that accomplishment of the mission and the welfare of all soldiers I come in contact with was the utmost reason why I was placed in the elite Non-commissioned Officer Corp. I love the Army and would not give up the past twenty years for nothing this world could offer me. These past twenty years coupled with the rearing that I received growing up, has made me the solid human being that I am today. I know that it sounds conceited at times, but the result achieved during these past twenty years speak for themselves. The one test of life is how strong you are when the odds are against you. When everything around you is crumbling down, what do you do when it seems to be no relief in sight. Faith is a powerful word and that is the one word that allowed me to stand here today. I have not been a smart soldier my entire career. At times, I seemed to be my own worst enemy. Doing the right thing is not always the most important thing for the question of "Are you the one to do the right thing?" Battles in this life are not always ours to fight. That was a hard lesson for me to learn. That leads back to what was the vision that I received from the Lord concerning my military career. He showed me a glimpse of the end: that I would retire after twenty years as an Sergeant First Class (E-7). What he did not show me was the fight and battles that would confront me during those years. In the fulfillment of that vision, there would be many of them. The vision I was shown was ironic in that it would be the only thing I had to hold on to at times during the past twenty years. It was a great source of comfort when the light looked dim and on the way to blowing out. There is nothing in this world that could compare to having all around you see the odds standing against you. Telling you that all you have worked so hard for what is about to be taken away from you in an instance. The greatest test of faith occurred about midway my twenty-year ordeal. I received a Quality Management Program (QMP) letter from the President of the Sergeant First Class (E-7) board. This came at a time when I was primed to get the promotion that had been promised by the father in my vision. After receiving the letter from my superior, I had a great dilemma on my hand that had to be dealt with during the next 72 hours. I had to make decisions that would affect my entire family. I had all kind of advice given during this time frame and most of it was contrary to what I had received within my vision. This entire episode was faced without any knowledge to my family. It was my battle, and yet, I knew that the outcome would affect all those who were close and dear to me. The very survival of life was on the line. I had nothing working for me but my faith in God and that was even looking dim at times. At times I would sit around and come up with various scenario of how I could survive in the midst of being out of the military. After two days of wrestling with the situation, I then went back to the vision and realized that this was only a distraction and I needed to fight like never before. The fight was about to begin and here is the rest of the story: I endured the test and December 1, 2000, I will be retired from a 20-year plus career. As you can see through this story it has not been an easy road to obtain this goal. Thanks to God it has been a joyous one through his grace and mercy. Praise GOD.

CHAPTER XXXIII

REVELATIONS: THE FINAL ANALYSIS

I often wondered why so many people failed to see me as a man. There had to be a reason behind that analysis. To say it was racism would be far from the truth. There had to be something that made them see only the "Black Man". One thing that came to mind was the fact that I often found myself in the role of an aggressive black man, which ultimately took their attention from the real "man". How enlightening yet disappointing it was to be known as a "Black Man" with an aggressive personality. I started to look at what the word aggression meant from other's point of view

Aggression #1

When you're rough, assertive, forceful, you're aggressive. Let's quickly move to the examples so that it can be explained better. I assume you probably know the game 'basketball'. Suppose a player went up to another who had the ball, and he tried to steal it from him. He shoves him hard and snatches the ball out of his hand. They will definitely call a foul on too much aggression. What I mean is that it wasn't necessary for the player to be so rough. He just needed to grab the ball as it came out of the other's hand. That's something else to add to the definition: unnecessary roughness. You can use aggression verbally, also. Suppose a friend has a handicap. You get into a fight with her, and she says, "I never liked you anyway!" You take this statement too hard and say, "I never liked you either, you handicapped cripple!" This would cut deep into the emotions of the opponent. You were showing much aggression by insulting your friend about something you knew she couldn't help.

There are some positives to aggression, though. You will need to have aggression if you have bullies. Think of it this way, if you are afraid of a bully, it's like you're the basketball, and your bully is the dribble. When he throws you around, instead of bouncing back to fend for yourself, you bounce away. Next time that dribbler feels like throwing you around, you bounce right back and show that dribbler just how it feels to be attacked. Don't take this the wrong way, though; don't push it too far. You're in a fight with someone. They claim you did something, even though you know you didn't do it. So you're probably thinking, I'm not going to let this guy *punk me in front of all my friends so you're wanting to beat him up, but you are just* getting yourself in deep trouble. Ask yourself this before a fight: Are my friends going to be there for me when I get suspended or expelled? Am I fighting to defend myself or just look good in front of someone else? You don't have to make this guy shed blood. Just do enough to defend yourself. Maybe a push or shove; get this guy on the ground. You don't want to be too aggressive in this situation, though, yet you need aggression to defend yourself.

There are probably more negatives to aggression. Your friend is angry with you for doing something. She's expressing her anger quietly so that she won't attract attention. The conversation gets louder and she lightly slaps you on the face. You can't even hear it. You get too worked up over this minor action and punch her so hard that you bust her lip and cause it to bleed. This shows, bluntly, that you have too much aggression. Aggression gets worked up from anger or maybe from taking little things too seriously. If you have a lot of aggression, then maybe you should try to calm yourself down so that you can work things out to be clean and orderly.

After looking at aggression from the mind of a twelve-year old, I began to see myself in a different light over the past 20 plus years in the United States Army. There were many times that I exhibited forcefulness when the actual situation did not call for the degree of it I demonstrated. The ideal of relating my actions with my superiors to that of a basketball game showed even more that I demonstrated a lot of unneeded assertion, forcefulness, and aggression that affected the other players in the game. There were many battles that I went head to head with my superiors that were not willing to fight. These aggressive moments, which were many and contributed to the others only seeing me as an aggressive black man. How absurd it was that the aggression I demonstrated towards my superiors, was never done toward my subordinates. Therefore I was walking what some would call separate lines in the United States Military. Over the years, I had become the basketball, and my superiors were dribbling me around the court. The end result of this was aggression, being shown in a negative way. It led to many loud and harsh words being exchanged between my superiors and me. The battle lines were drawn and it seemed as though neither side would give up any ground or leverage to the other. It often led to a very unhealthy environment.

The fact that there was a "Man" in the midst of all this aggression was lost due to the very word itself "aggression. I had allowed myself to be drawn into an aggressive state of mind and therefore many aggressive acts were done over the course of 20 plus years. Yet, the "Man" in me was still going about my daily business taking care of soldiers and their needs. One would ask how could these two co-exist at the same time? The answer is rather simple when you look at the facts. First of all the aggressiveness only came out when I felt threatened, or my pride was being insulted by those who had authority over me. Secondly, that aggression with my superiors led to the quality of service that the soldiers and their families received from me as a supervisor of the PAC. Thirdly, I sort of inherited the responsibility of being the tough guy with all my superiors until it became a way of life. Therefore, soldiers grew to love me as a soldier and a man with a backbone. On the other hand, most of my superiors just saw me as an aggressive black man on the loose. In the latter days of my United States Army career, I began to learn how to balance out my aggression and started to define myself as a man more and more. The first 15 years of my military career was full of forceful aggressiveness. While my last five years were full of toned-down aggression and a lot of coaching and acting as a mentor soldiers. It was through this acting as a mentor and coaching that I began to see myself in a new light. For it was the very things that I told them to refrain from, I had been performing over the years. It seemed as though I was seeing my own mistakes through the acting as a mentor and coaching of others. Therefore I had to learn not to be a man of aggression, yet display aggressiveness, if the need arose for it. Aggression is not bad when used at the right time. During the first 15 years of my career, I was a very aggressive soldier because I was always on the defensive side of the ball game. Therefore, aggression was all I knew. When the offense came at me in the form of my superiors, I just hit them hard with much aggressiveness.

Aggression#2

Aggression is the act of attacking, or taking the offensive position.

Aggression is a word that one can mold into different meanings when one refers to an action or position. This trait, or flaw, can lead to great things, or lead to things that hatred has driven. Many people say that aggression is a quality that everyone should possess. However, one must use this quality responsibly. Aggression may seem as a quality to others. Nevertheless, it can be a weakness, or character flaw to some. This quality can be a sign of pride and drive to achieve something no matter what the costs may be. Many people find themselves aggressive in their workplace because they see this as a way to obtain certain objectives such as: a pay raise, a promotion to an executive level, or a way to find favor in the boss' eye. These people will jump at any chance to participate or use an event, strategy, or invention as a way to the top. They will use their aggressive trait to push them to the max of the objective and will feed off the inner drive not to let anything, or anyone, stop them. Unfortunately, this is the point where aggression can lead others to deeds that they would not think to do. Had it not been for this asset to become a trait of impassive disregard for what is ethically right, aggressive people would not be so prone to bend to it.

The example of the workplace will also fit into this mold of aggression. At some point, aggression can become something that can be hard to control when one wants something so badly, that they don't care how they get it. This is where people begin to plot on how to rid themselves of any problem or hindrance to the accomplishment of their objective. A person whose aggressive nature becomes they catch the dictator of that person's actions up in the web that can lead to many disastrous things. For example, people whose job requires a little aggression to a certain extent. Sometimes, a person is so committed to making a name for them, that they will do anything to get the story. These are the ones whose job and inner being can lead to take on an aggressive nature to get what they want. They will look for a way to achieve that goal and will not rest until they get that objective that they feel will set their career off. They will override any authority, setting himself or herself above anyone in a command position. For, in their minds, a person in a command over them is a hindrance to their objective. In their minds, that person is only trying to keep them from reaching it. They will show blatant disregard for ethics and the natural rights of others. The person will harass, injure, wrongfully discredit, and sometimes, extort others to get the objective that they are seeking. This kind of aggression is a poison to the mind and soul. The person has become someone that is completely different in every aspect. Their actions may soon become heartless; their mind incoherent to moral values. The aggression consumes their life that has embedded itself into their heart. The person will look to their aggressive nature for the answer to all their problems. To them, nothing is impossible to obtain without their aggressive nature finding a way to get it. Aggression is a word with many meanings. No matter the meaning, aggression has a moral use and an immoral use of it. One cannot teach aggression. One can only breed it within the minds of people. An aggressive nature is within everyone. Those who choose to water the seed are those that decide to eat and drink the kind of fruit it will bear.

Through all of that aggression that I kept hitting them with brought the life the aggression through the mind of a seventeen-year old young man. It talks about aggression from the act of attacking and taking the offensive position. That was the response of my superiors in my early years in the Army. Over the years our relationship had molded into one of aggression filled with traits that were flowed to the point of hatred at times. This kind of aggression only led to acts that showed no regard for right or wrong. It was obvious that I knew where I wanted to go, and at all cost, I was going to get there. The unique thing about where I wanted to go,, was that it was a positive accomplishment. This problem with where I was going, was that the aggression bouts between my superiors and I had grown so bitter that it did not matter whether it was good, bad, right or wrong, positive or negative. They were just set on stopping me from getting there. This was never more obvious then during the years of 1989 through 1992 at the Special Forces Training Group. I wanted so badly to start the SPAC from scratch. I was as determined that I would let no one deter me from that cause. Anyone or anything that tried to hinder its conception felt the harsh aggression from me. Meanwhile, my superiors had another goal in mind. That goal was to get me out of the Special Forces Training Community for good. There, we had two objectives that were being sought at the same time. You would think that there would have been some room for both, yet the truth is there was not. The aggression was strong from both fronts, yet there were different types of aggression. The reason for that was that the desires were of two different calibers. I wanted to accomplish something positive and they wanted to accomplish something negative. Therefore, the rules for aggression were different for each side. First, let us look at the superiors' goal for a moment. It was clear from the start: I had to go. This would lead them to do anything for completion, injure my reputation, discredit me as a soldier and at times, extort others to work with this to accomplish this goal. That alone would lead me through some disastrous times. At first, it was get him away from the Command during the first three years. This all of a sudden all the rules changed. The aggression grew to the point where the superiors suddenly became consumed, and lost all concepts of moral values. That was when they tried to rid the United States Army of me through the Quality Management Program. Ultimately, they got the mission completed as I departed the command in October 1992.

WHY DID I HAVE TO FIGHT SO HARD?

Over 20 years, I felt that I had to fight for everything that I achieved. It all started many years before I joined the United States Army. Nothing ever came easy to our community as we grew up. There always was something going on and we constantly had to strive to overcome the obstacles. It had become a part of my life and despite all the great achievements I attained during my career, the fight continued to the very end. I often wondered why it seemed so hard, yet it all seemed simple from the start. I had been chosen to live out a dream and vision given to me by God. Knowing that gave me the belief that it was not going to be an easy road. I often made my road a rougher one by trying to make the crooked road straight on my own. I had placed the responsibility on my shoulder of bringing the dream and vision to pass. The truth of the matter in that I was only the vessel and God was the one who would bring it to pass. All I knew was that I had to fight my way through any obstacle that got in my way. It was not until the year of 1992 that I began to realize that the battle was not mines, but God's. It took the opposition trying to take it all for me to see that I was just the vessel for God. He wanted to demonstrate his awesome power through me. I was interfering with his handy work by walking in my wisdom of what was really happening. For years, I was a vessel of sort to the vision that God had given me. After 1992, I still had to fight hard with a different fight: this fight was against myself. The fight was to stay out of the way and let God have his way. I had to learn the hard way that what was in my early years, was no more in my later years. Times had changed and I was still living in the time of old. The road that I traveled in the last 9 years of my career were full of plots to overthrow me, but I did not have to fight as hard because I had learned that the fight was not mines.

The one thing that I desired from the start of this adventure within the United States Army was being recognized as an INDIVIDUAL. To have yourself categorized within a group takes away from the differences that can be made as an individual. The respect that I experienced through being different made many of the battles I faced daily worth it. As I entered each new unit the word was clearly out that this soldier is not a team player in the sense that he speaks what he believes regardless. That made many enemies, but at the same time made me know that the desire to be who I was, ME was still alive. As I departed that great organization I left as I entered: A man who others will always just see as a black man. Each time I would find myself in the midst of a battle, I allowed my soldiers to go through them with me. Each time the enemy declared that this would be the end of the Black Man's career within the United States Army. Hope is what the battles I won gave the young soldiers whom so gallantly cheered for me in the midst of no hope as they saw it. When soldiers see a leader who does the right thing beat the odds, it gives them hope that doing the right will pay off after all. I have met many of those soldiers who have served with me as far as 1985 and they all stand amazed that I retired from the Military. To add to that amazement they show me their retirement Identification Card and that makes all that I went through worth while. The products that have stemmed from the hostile environments in which I served have demonstrated the tenacity to hang in there when all seemed worthless. Many of them tell me they have a few years to go and I encourage them to hang in there for there is no greater feeling than to be retired from the Armed Forces. The hard fights that this Man from Monticello, Florida was an extension of the many days I battled the farm, heat and all other obstacles that farm life brought. It was those fights in my rearing days that carried over into the battles I fought daily within the United States Army. The endurance and stability to see the battle until the end was already instilled and all that was left to do was run the course until the end. The valuable training that I received from the heart of the country has led me into a deeper appreciation for the small things of life and taught me how to be a true warrior no matter how tough the battle.

Just imagine yourself in the midst of a battle going on and your mentor and coach has been targeted for elimination. You have depended on this coach and mentor for all you have achieved thus far. You have the inner desire to help, but there is nothing you can really do but watch the fight and hope in the end the mentor and coach wins. The amazing thing about the mentor and coach is that in the midst of the battle he is still mentoring and coaching you daily. You wonder where he gets his strength and endurance to go on from. Early in the fight it seems that each round goes against him and still to the amazement of you his strength and endurance is getting stronger by the round. Then all of a sudden when it all seems to be caving in on the mentor and coach something unique happens, the tide of the fight changes and the opposition seems to be stunned for the rest of the fight. After each battle during the after action review the antidote for success is revealed time and time again by the mentor and coach. You must become the absolute expert in all that you attempt to do, and it is that knowledge, wisdom and understanding that will allow winning the battle in the end. During the early rounds you allow the opponent to lay his cards on the table and in the later rounds you discredit them one by one. Always remember those who are swift to take you out, very seldom do their homework before they enter the battle. They are so consumed with the end result that they will have a game plan for the fight that is full of holes. Those holes are where being the absolute expert will allow you to win every time. Many commands tried to eliminate this Black Man through the Overweight Program and came up short on this hole. "Health Care Provider clearing the mentor and coach for entry into an Overweight Program" *Some wonder why it was so important that I have endured so many fights and did it ever occur to me I could have lost? With the Dream and Vision being alive within me from God I now know it was my endurance and strength to hold on to the Dream and Vision that allowed victory to come each time they were attacked. If I had any point just threw in the towel and conceded to the many attacks, it would have been I who lost not God.*

The fight was worth it because whether they saw me as a "Man" or a "Black Man" they all knew as an individual I stood up for what I believed to be right and God.

WHO WON?

When it was all over, one would ask who won the ball game. Well, first of all, one would have to look at the players in the game. After looking at the subordinates in the game, you must know that they were the beneficiaries of some top-notch administrative services. Many careers were served through the territory of me to speak what I felt to be right. My willingness to stand alone many times gave them new leases on life in the United States Army. Now, to the superiors that worked under my supervision, they experienced the greatest support system that one soldier could offer. I took care of their units, my ordeals, and ensured that they were productive within the abilities they contained. Many times, I was asked to penalize them for their shortcomings and I refused. Therefore, they were beneficiary to the ball game, also. Now, to my peers, they got to sit at ringside and see the odd soldier of the bunch torment many supervisors during the many confrontations over the past 20 years. The feeling in the air said, Get ready for some excitement, for the oddball of the bunch has arrived. What a benefit they enjoyed during a hotheaded meeting.

The lower-echelon supervisors would have to be the players in the ball game that endured some hard times over the past 20 years. It was them who had the arduous task of controlling the wild administrator on the loose. Many times during the process, there were many day-to-day meetings that left them frustrated with the end results of the meeting. Not all was bad for them, in that they enjoyed the many achievements by this out of control administrator. The achievements were the key to a lot of them learning how to allow their soldiers to do what they were good at Administration. Once they realized this, all things were smooth sailing for them as long as they stayed true to that course of action.

The life of the higher-echelon of superiors proved to be the greatest beneficiary of it all. Through all of the rough times that all the others players in the game experienced, none were really felt at this level. All the great achievements in what the higher-echelon of superiors enjoyed. From the start, they got the awesome abilities and achievements of the "absolute expert". With all the great benefits received by the higher-echelon superiors, they were far from the winners in the ball game. The supervisors would have to be the most battered players in this wild ball game that was being played. The responsibilities that came with this position were more than any one man could handle. All of them had to leave the ball game many times to go see the sideline physician.

During many of these visits, they were placed on the injured-reserve list for a while. Bruised, battered, and almost out for the kill, most of them still managed to survive to the end of the game. So, in the end, even they were the benefactors of the great achievements during each era. So, why is this question so hard to answer? You would think that you have figured out who the winner is because there is only one player left in the game. Well, let us take a look at that last player in the game: ME. I endured a lot of hardships, pain, setbacks and other obstacles over my long career in the United States Army. I was tested to the limit with each obstacle I faced. I almost lost it all through a major conspiracy to rid the United States Army of the likes of me. I had many bouts with depression, anxieties, and other emotions that almost took me out. Yet, in the midst of it all, I was able to achieve many great accomplishments. The achievements were a clear demonstration of my ability to work under pressure. All being said and done, I had endured 20 years and four months of duty in the United States Army. The benefits of this tour was a new status of a "Retiree from One of the Greatest Organizations you could ever serve With: The United States Army". As that effective date of retirement came to pass on December 1, 2000, all the anxieties and other adversities faced in the United States Army took on a new meaning. It was like a great weight had been lifted off my shoulders. Finally, the dream and vision had been completed. What a road that had been traveled to accomplish such an awesome task. Still, I was not the winner of the ball game. We all had benefited in one way or another. On the other hand, we have also endured many hard times. So, who won? Well, let us focus on the one person we have not mentioned at all during this search for an answer: The Coach. He was never a player in the ball game, but he had all the players under his control. He was there from the start and was deeply involved in every play that occurred during the whole tour of duty. He was there holding me up during the hard times that I encountered as his words in fulfilling the vision and dream that he had given me before I entered the United States Army. During the deep states of depression, and there were many during my tour do duty, there was always someone there to aid me in overcoming it. I now realized that it was through those times that I got many encouraging words that made me who I am today. God has always been there aiding this vessel in overcoming many tribulations that have brought to pass this vision and dream.

So, the winner in this whole ordeal that I've faced over my military career is God. To him be all the glory, for all he has done for me. Without him by my side, I could have achieved none of the great achievements. It took all of those who aided me by their actions to bring me to the point where I am today. It showed me what I was made of and also prepared me for what I was ordained to do from the foundation of the world: Share the Person I am with the World. To include the good, bad, ugly, beauty, shortfalls, weaknesses, strengths, lows, high, and all the other things that make me who I am. I owe my entire life to him and that is why I am committed to showing others that it takes all the things within them to make them who they are. Many times, I felt that those things made me a bad person until I realized that it took all of it to make me who I am today: ME.

Praise God, for all he has done within my life as his vessel.

THE END OF IT ALL

The below left picture shows a young man that grew up in the heart of the country. During those years he learned how to survive in settings many only hear of. For the entire 18 years of his life at home he visited the outdoor toilet night after night, not knowing what it was like to grow up with an inside one. He spent many days gathering up firewood to ensure that the house was warm enough to be comfortable. Starting fires was his chore first thing in the morning for five years. Growing up with nine brothers and sisters would lead him into the ultimate responsibility of ensuring that all assigned tasking were complete as the oldest child for five years. The farm was his way of life and it consumed much of his time during the planting season. The work ethic was always enforced and there was no doubt that I was ready to work hard no matter where I chose to go afterwards. Overall my life was consumed with the following: Peas, Beans, Okra, Washpots, Rubboards, Clothes pins, Clothes lines, Mules, Turn plows, hogs, chickens, ducks, hoes, weeds, hampers, watermelons fields, and work. It was through all of this that the young man from the heart of the country embarked on an adventure in the United States Army. He left with the desire to make his mark as a Man and not just be remembered as a Black Man that served his country.

The above right picture shows a young man who entered this world from the heart of the country and had to learn how to survive. He quickly had to adjust to racism, discrimination and most of all a versatile group of people who were well advance in dealing with the More Advance World. Each day he had to make quick adjustments just to keep up with the growing stages of adulthood in the United States Army. Some days were known as lesson learners of the harshest caliper. He endured foreign countries where his ability to stay the course was tested beyond measures. He had a dream and vision and it took all within him to stay true to it, with all the attacks and opposition he faced during the completion of it. He had to deal with a society of people who felt that the color of his skin did not allow him to be accepted at times for the contents of his abilities as a man. Each endeavor that he attempted to accomplish was met with strong opposition because of a choice he made in his tenure of duty: Transformation and not Conformation. His desire to be who he was made life a living hell for him at times. His story is full of Pains, Heartaches, Attitudes, Obstacles, Schemes, Personal Vengeance, Racism, and Discrimination. Yet he stands with the mission completed as a Man known to others as just a Black Man